word
edward peppitt

For over 60 years, more than 40
million people have learnt over
750 subjects the **teach yourself**
way, with impressive results.

be where you want to be
with **teach yourself**

For UK orders: please contact Bookpoint Ltd., 130 Milton Park, Abingdon, Oxon OX14 4SB. Telephone: +44 (0)/1235 827720. Fax: +44 (0)/1235 400454. Lines are open 09.00–18.00, Monday to Saturday, with a 24-hour message answering service. You can also order through our website www.teachyourself.co.uk

For USA order enquiries: please contact McGraw-Hill Customer Services, PO Box 545, Blacklick, OH 43004-0545, USA. Telephone: 1-800-722-4726. Fax: 1-614-755-5645.

For Canada order enquiries: please contact McGraw-Hill Ryerson Ltd., 300 Water St, Whitby, Ontario L1N 9B6, Canada. Telephone: 905 430 5000. Fax: 905 430 5020.

Long renowned as the authoritative source for self-guided learning – with more than 40 million copies sold worldwide – the *Teach Yourself* series includes over 300 titles in the fields of languages, crafts, hobbies, business, computing and education.

British Library Cataloguing in Publication Data A catalogue record for this title is available from The British Library.

Library of Congress Catalog Card Number: On file.

First published in UK 2003 by Hodder Headline Plc., 338 Euston Road, London, NW1 3BH.

First published in US 2003 by Contemporary Books, A Division of The McGraw-Hill Companies, 1 Prudential Plaza, 130 East Randolph Street, Chicago, Illinois 60601 USA.

The 'Teach Yourself' name is a registered trade mark of Hodder & Stoughton Ltd. Computer hardware and software brand names mentioned in this book are protected by their respective trademarks and are acknowledged.

 Typeset by MacDesign, Southampton

Printed in Great Britain for Hodder & Stoughton Educational, a division of Hodder Headline Plc, 338 Euston Road, London NW1 3BH by Cox & Wyman Ltd., Reading, Berkshire.

Papers used in this book are natural, renewable and recyclable products. They are made from wood grown in sustainable forests. The logging and manufacturing processes conform to the environmental regulations of the country of origin.

Impression number   10 9 8 7 6 5 4 3 2 1

Year   2007 2006 2005 2004 2003

contents

01

getting started

Start Word

1 Click .

2 Point to **Programs**.

3 Select **Microsoft Word**.

Or

1 Double click Microsoft Word on your desktop.

Close Word

1 Click on ✖ in top right-hand corner of screen.

Or

2 In the **File** menu, select **Exit**.

3 Save your document(s) if you are prompted to do so.

Move around text using the keyboard

There are four keystroke combinations that will enable you to navigate around a document quickly.

[Ctrl] + [Home] takes you straight to the beginning of the document.

[Ctrl] + [End] takes you straight to the end of the document.

[Ctrl] + [Pg Up] takes you to the top of the preceding page.

[Ctrl] + [Pg Dn] takes you to the top of the next page.

Use keyboard shortcuts

There are keyboard shortcuts for most of the common commands in Word. We have chosen not to list the keyboard equivalent for all the instructions in this book, but you can learn many of the shortcuts by looking through the drop-down main menus.

Use scrollbars

Scrollbars provide another means of navigating through a document.

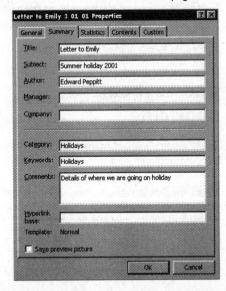

- Scroll up
- Click and drag
- Scroll down
- Previous page
- Select object
- Next page

Set file properties

You can set file properties to make it easier to find or sort documents at a later date.

1 In the **File** menu, select **Properties**.

2 You can summarize your document by entering data for title, subject, categories, keywords and comments.

Letter to Emily 3 01 01 Properties

General | Summary | Statistics | Contents | Custom

Title: Letter to Emily

Subject: Summer holiday 2001

Author: Edward Peppitt

Manager:

Company:

Category: Holidays

Keywords: Holidays

Comments: Details of where we are going on holiday

Hyperlink base:

Template: Normal

☐ Save preview picture

OK   Cancel

Replace text by highlighting

1 Highlight the text that you want to replace.

2 Type in the new text.

Replace text using overtype mode

1 Move cursor to where you want to replace text.

2 Double-click OVR on the Status bar.

3 Start typing. As you type, the text ahead will be overwritten.

Delete single character

1 To delete the character to the right of the cursor, press **[Del]**.

2 To delete the character to the left, press **[Backspace]**.

Delete text

1 Highlight the text that you want to delete.

2 Press the **[Del]** key or the **[Backspace]** key.

Select text using the mouse

To select a word, double-click the word.

To select a range of text, click and hold while dragging the mouse over the text.

To select a line:

Move the mouse into the left margin until the cursor changes to inward-pointing arrow. Click once.

To select a paragraph:

Move the mouse into the left margin until the cursor changes to inward-pointing arrow. Click twice.

To select all the text:

Move the mouse into the left margin until the cursor changes to inward-pointing arrow. Click three times.

De-select text

- Click anywhere within the text

Or

- Press one of the arrow keys

Drag and drop text (move)

You can move text around a document using the drag and drop feature:

1 Highlight the text to be moved.
2 Click on highlighted text and drag to desired position.
3 Release the mouse button.

Drag and drop text (copy)

1 Highlight the text to be copied.
2 Hold down the **[Ctrl]** key, click on the highlighted text and drag to the desired position.
3 Release the mouse button.

Cut text

1 Highlight the text to be cut.

2 Click .

Copy text

1 Highlight the text to be copied.

2 Click .

Paste text

1 Move the cursor to where text will be inserted.

2 Click .

tip

There are keyboard shortcuts to make cut, copy and paste
even quicker:
[Ctrl] and [X] = cut
[Ctrl] and [C] = copy
[Ctrl] and [V] = paste

Make two or more copy selections

1 In the **View** menu, select **Task Pane**.
2 Click on the down arrow at the top of the **Task Pane** and select **Clipboard**.
3 Highlight the first copy selection, then click in the main toolbar.
4 Highlight the next selection, then click .
5 Each selection will be displayed in the Task Pane, as well as thumbnails of any cut or copied images. You can make up to 24 selections.
6 Move the cursor to where you want to paste and click on the selection in the **Task Pane** to insert it.

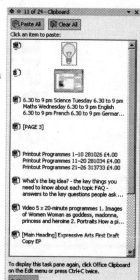

tip

You can also use the Clipboard in the Task Pane to copy content between Microsoft Office software applications.

02

screen display

Change the way a document is displayed

Word offers a number of ways of viewing your document. Click on the appropriate icon in the bottom left-hand of your screen.

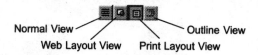

Normal View — Outline View
Web Layout View — Print Layout View

Display toolbars

1 In the **View** menu, select **Toolbars**.
2 Click on any toolbar name to display it.

Create more working space by switching off any toolbars that you are not using.

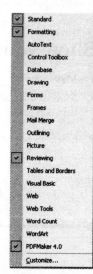

Hide white space

In Word 2002, you can save screen space by hiding white space at the top and bottom of each page in **Print Layout View**.

1 Make sure that you are in **Print Layout View** (see page 11).

2 Move the cursor to the grey space between pages shown on the screen.

3 Click .

Show white space

1 Make sure that you are in **Print Layout View** (see page 11).

2 Move the cursor to the black line indicating the space between pages on the screen.

3 Click .

Display ruler

1 In the **View** menu, select **Ruler**.

Click to display ruler

Switch to full screen display

To create more working space, switch to full screen display. All toolbars and menus are hidden from view, devoting the full screen to your working document.

1 In the **View** menu, select **Full Screen**.
2 Click **Close Full Screen** to revert to the previous view.

Use full screen

Use Zoom

The Zoom facility allows you to alter the size of the document as it is displayed on your screen. It does not alter the final printed document.

1 In the **View** menu, select **Zoom**.

2 Choose a Zoom option.

3 Click **OK**.

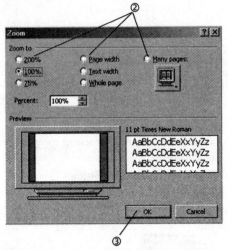

Turn on/off dynamic menus

In Word 2002, drop-down menus only display the most commonly used options for the first few seconds. After a brief pause, menus expand automatically to show all available commands.

When first opened

Fully open

You can click the down arrows to open the menu

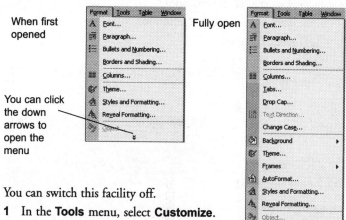

You can switch this facility off.

1 In the **Tools** menu, select **Customize**.
2 Click on **Options** tab.
3 Tick **Always show full menus**.
4 Click **Close**.

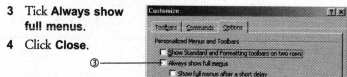

Turn on/off dynamic toolbars

Word 2002 saves desktop space by combining the Standard and Formatting toolbars on a single line, and displaying only those icons that are commonly used.

You can switch this facility off.

1 In the **Tools** menu, select **Customize**.
2 Click on **Options** tab.
3 Place a tick where indicated.
4 Click **Close**.

Tick here to keep the Standard and Formatting toolbars separate

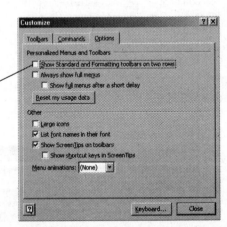

View Task Pane

The Task Pane is a new feature in
Word 2002, which provides shortcuts
to common tasks and processes.

1 In the **View** menu, select **Task
Pane**.

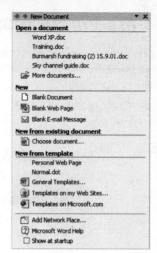

The Task pane, here displaying
the New Document options

Use the Task Pane
shortcut menus

1 Click the downward-pointing
arrow at the top of the Task Pane.

2 Select the appropriate shortcut
menu.

Personalize menus and toolbars

There are a number of ways in which you can customize the menus and toolbars that you use in Word.

1 In the **Tools** menu, select **Customize**.

2 Click on each of the tabs to see the customization options available.

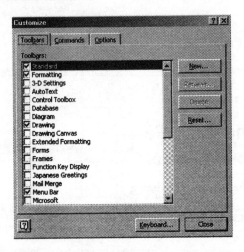

Customize toolbars

Customize menus

Other Customization options

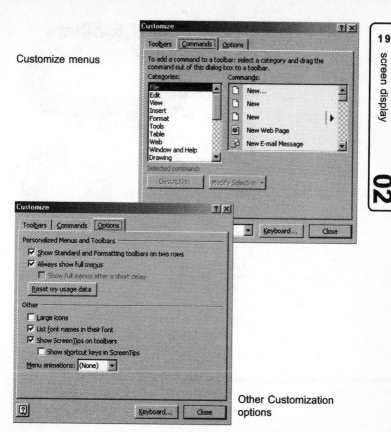

03

new documents

Create a new blank document

1 Start Word.

2 A new blank document will appear automatically.

Or

1 Click **Start**.

2 Select **New Office Document**.

3 Select **Blank document**.

4 Click **OK**.

Or

1 Make sure the Task Pane is displayed.

2 In the Task Pane, select **Blank Document**.

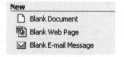

Create a new document using a template

1 In the **File** menu, select **New**.
2 Select an appropriate template type where indicated.
3 Click on the tab for the type of document that you want to create.
4 Select a template.
5 Click **OK**.

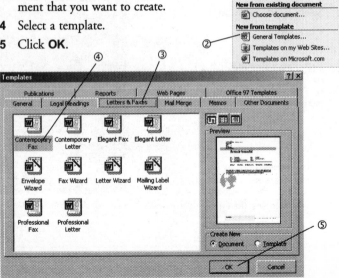

Create a letter using Letter Wizard

1 Open a new blank document, or another suitable document template.

2 In the **Tools** menu, point to **Letters and Mailings**, and select **Letter Wizard**.

3 Follow the wizard's step-by-step instructions.

4 Click **OK**.

5 When the wizard has finished, you can amend or adjust the letter to suit your requirements.

Work through the tabs in turn

Click to see the design choices

Click to see the style options

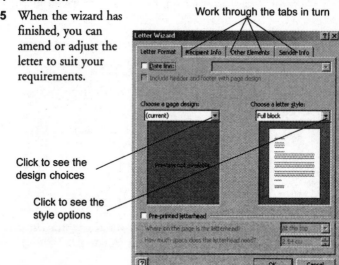

Create new documents using wizards

1 In the **File** menu, select **New**.
2 Click to select **General Templates**.
3 Click the tab containing the wizard you want to use.
4 Click to select the wizard.
5 Click **OK**.
6 Follow the Wizard's instructions to create your own document.

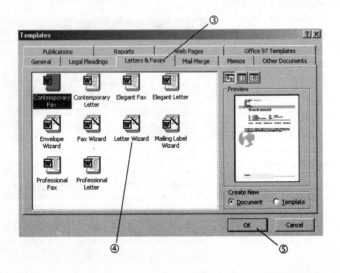

Save a document for the first time

1 Click 🖫 on the Standard toolbar.
2 Navigate to the folder where you wish to store the document.
3 Give the document a meaningful name.
4 Click **Save**.

Save a document again

You should remember to save your document at regular intervals in one of the following ways:

- Click 🖫 at any time.
- In the **File** menu, select **Save**.
- Hold down **[Ctrl]** and press **[S]**.

Save a document as a different file type

1 In the **File** menu, select **Save As**.
2 Click on the down arrow next to **Save as type**.
3 Select the appropriate file type.
4 Click **Save**.

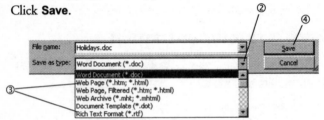

Save a copy of a document

1 Open the document that you want to copy.
2 In the **File** menu, select **Save As**.
3 Navigate to the folder where you want to store the copy.
4 Rename the document.
5 Click **Save**.

Protect a document with a password

1 Open the document that you want to protect.
2 In the **File** menu, select **Save As**.
3 In the **Tools** drop-down menu, select **Security Options**.
4 Type a password in the **Password to open** box.

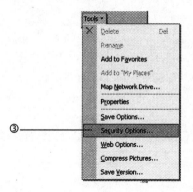

You can also prevent a document from being modified with a
password. Repeat steps 1–8, but this time enter the password
in the **Password to Modify** field.

5 Click **OK**.

6 Type the password again in the **Re-enter password to open** box.

7 Click **OK**.

8 Click **Save**.

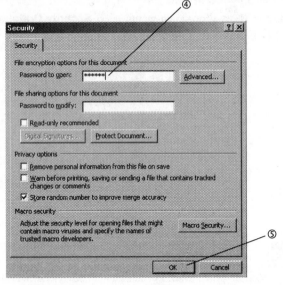

Change how often Word saves documents automatically

1 In the **Tools** menu, select **Options**.
2 Click on the **Save** tab.
3 Adjust the **AutoRecovery** time where indicated.
4 Click **OK**.

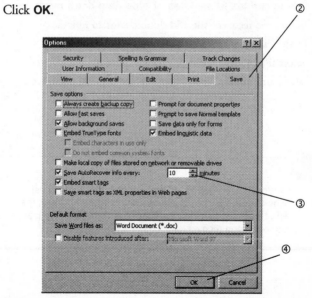

Recover a document that was saved automatically

1 In the **File** menu, select **Open**.

2 Navigate to the folder containing recovered files. This is usually **Windows\Application Data\Microsoft\Word**

3 Select **All Files** in the **Files of type** drop-down menu.

4 Locate the recovery file and double-click to open it.

5 In the **File** menu, select **Save**.

6 Select the original name for the document.

7 When prompted, agree to replace the existing document.

tip

In Word XP, you can often recover documents that crash.
When you restart Word after a system failure or crash, the
File Recovery pane will be displayed, listing the files that you
can open and recover.

Let Word create a backup copy of a document

1 In the **File** menu, select **Save As**.
2 Click on **Tools** and select **Save Options**.
3 Place a tick in the **Always create backup copy** check box.
4 Click **OK**.
5 Click **Save**.

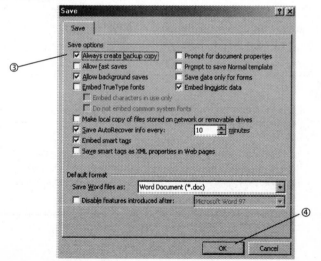

Open a document

1 Click .

Or

In the **File** menu, select **Open**.

2 Navigate to the folder containing the document you want to open.

3 Double-click on the document.

Or

Click once on the document and then click ⟨ Open ⟩.

tip

If you want to open a document that you have worked on recently, you may see it listed at the foot of the **File** menu. If so, just click on it.

Find a document

It is very easy to forget where on your hard disk you have saved a
document. If this happens to you:

1 Click **Start** and select **Search**, then **For Files or Folders**.
2 Enter the name of the document, or a part of it.
3 Add any data that might assist the search into the appropriate
   fields (e.g. a date range or some keywords contained in the text).
4 Click **Search Now**.
5 Files matching the search criteria will be listed. Double-click on
   the file name to open it.

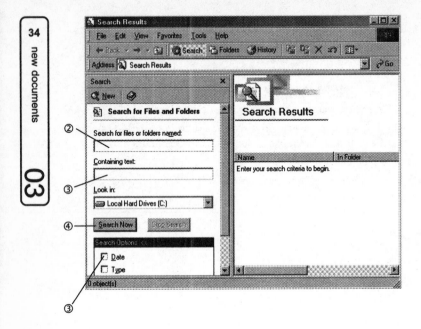

printing

04

Print a whole document

Click 🖨 or hold down **[Ctrl]** and press **[P]**.

Print part of a document

1 In the **File** menu, select **Print**.
2 Select the **Page range**.
3 Click **OK**.

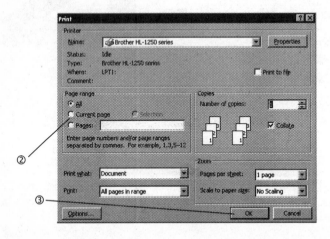

Change print criteria

1 In the **File** menu, select **Print**.

You can:

- Select the print range.
- Specify the number of copies to print.
- Select scale or zoom.
- Select odd or even pages only.

Switch to a different printer

1 In the **File** menu, select **Print**.
2 Click on the down arrow next to **Printer Name**.
3 Select a printer.

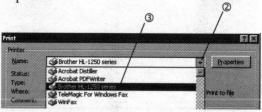

Edit printer properties

1 In the **File** menu, select **Print**.
2 Click on **Properties**.
3 Select the desired options.
4 Click **OK**.

Scroll through the tabs for other print options

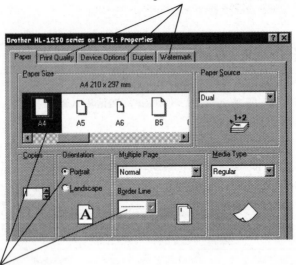

Select the options

Preview a document before printing

1 Click 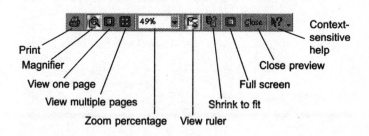.

Or

- In the **File** menu, select **Print Preview**.
2 Click **Close** to return to the previous view.

Adjust print preview settings

1 Select the appropriate option from the Print Preview toolbar.
2 Use the scrollbar to navigate between previewed pages.

Print
Magnifier
View one page
View multiple pages
Zoom percentage View ruler
Shrink to fit
Full screen
Close preview
Context-sensitive help

Alter the page setup

1 In the **File** menu, select **Page Setup**.

2 Alter the Margins, Paper size and source and Layout settings as required.

3 Click **OK** when finished.

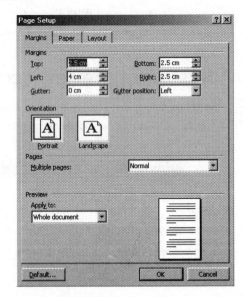

The margins options

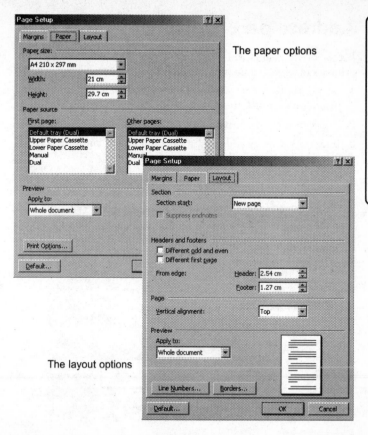

The paper options

The layout options

Address an envelope

If your printer allows you to feed envelopes through it then you can
print an address directly onto the envelope.

1 In the **Tools** menu, point to **Letters and Mailings**, and select
  Envelopes and Labels.

2 Click to select the **Envelopes** tab.

3 Enter the delivery address if it does not appear automatically.

4 Enter a return address if applicable.

5 Click **Print** if you want to print the envelope on its own.

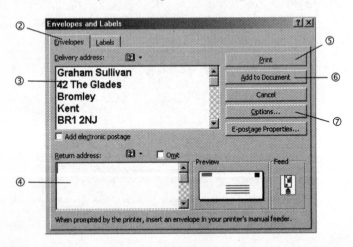

6 Click **Add to Document** if you want to print the envelope at the same time as the complete document.

7 Click **Options** to change the envelope printing options.

8 Click to select the **Envelope Options** tab.

9 Make changes as desired.

10 Click **OK**.

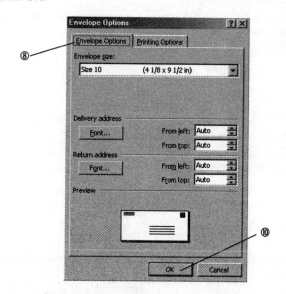

Print two pages on a single sheet

1 In the **File** menu, select **Page Setup**.

2 Click to select the **Margins** tab.

3 Select **2 pages per sheet** from the **Multiple pages** menu.

4 Click **OK**.

When you are ready to print your document, use any of the normal methods (see page 36).

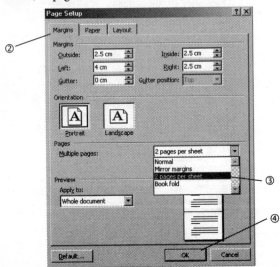

Print multiple pages on a single sheet

In Word, you can print thumbnails of the pages of a document on a single sheet

1 In the **File** menu, select **Print**.

2 Click to select the desired number of pages per sheet.

3 Click **OK**.

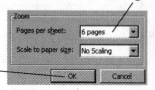

Shrink text to fit a single page

Sometimes a document will not quite fit onto a single page. Word can automatically shrink the document so that it fits neatly onto a single page.

1 Click .

2 Click 📑.

3 Click **Close**.

tip

You can also use this method to shrink three pages into two.

Include a watermark in your document

1 In the Format menu, point to Background and select Printed Watermark .

2 Choose either a picture or a text Watermark where indicated.

3 Select the picture or choose text as appropriate.

4 Click Apply .

5 Click OK.

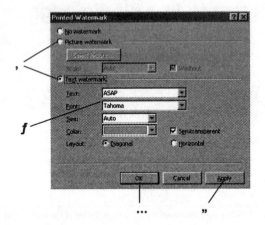

05

formatting

Set character spacing

1 Highlight the characters or words that you want to space.
2 In the **Format** menu, select **Font**.
3 Click on the **Character Spacing** tab.
4 Select the character spacing and position.
5 Click **OK**.

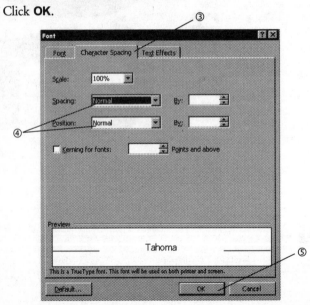

Set line/paragraph spacing

1 Highlight the lines or paragraphs that you want to space.

2 In the **Format** menu, select **Paragraph**.

3 Make a selection in the **Line spacing** field.

4 Click **OK**.

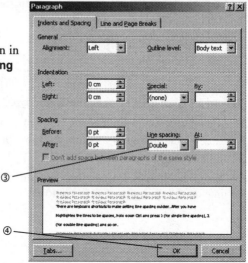

tip

There are keyboard shortcuts for line spacing. Highlight the lines to be spaced, then hold down **[Ctrl]** and press **[1]** (for single line spacing), **[2]** (for double line spacing) and so on.

Use bold/italic/underline

1 Highlight the text that you want to change.

2 Click on the appropriate icon in the formatting toolbar.

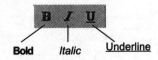

Bold *Italic* <u>Underline</u>

You can set bold, italic or underline as you type:

1 Move cursor to the point where you want to type.

2 Click on the appropriate icon in the formatting toolbar.

3 Begin typing.

4 To turn bold, italic or underline off again, click for a second time on the appropriate toolbar button.

Change typeface/font or text size

1 Highlight the text that you want to change.
2 Select an appropriate font or typeface from the drop-down menus.

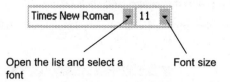

Open the list and select a
font

Font size

If you want to incorporate a number of different typefaces and
text sizes, you may find it easier to introduce a document
Style into your documents (see page 76).

Change font formatting

There are other changes you can make to the way text looks:

1 Highlight the text that you want to change.
2 In the **Format** menu, select **Font**.
3 Make the appropriate changes and click **OK**.

You can set the font, font style and size, and simple effects, like a text shadow or outline.

Click on **Text Effects** to set other special effects like text that blinks or sparkles.

Set special effects

Define the font and style

Align text

1 Highlight the text that you want to align.
2 Click on the appropriate icon in the formatting toolbar.

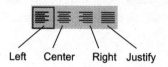

Left   Center   Right   Justify

Align text as you type

1 Move cursor to the point where you want to type.
2 Click on the appropriate icon in the formatting toolbar.
3 Text will be aligned accordingly from this point forward.

Copy formatting with the Format Painter

The Format Painter allows you to copy the formatting of a word, sentence or paragraph, and apply it to another part of a document.

1 Highlight the words or characters whose formatting you want to copy.

2 Click ⬦.

3 Click and drag the mouse over the text that you want to format.

4 Release the mouse.

You can copy the formatting for an entire paragraph:

1 Click ¶ to display the paragraph marks.

2 Highlight the paragraph mark at the end of the paragraph whose formatting you want to copy.

3 Click ⬦.

4 Click and drag the mouse over paragraph mark at the end of the paragraph that you want to format.

5 Release the mouse.

Select all text in a document with the same formatting

1 Click on 🔏 on the Formatting toolbar to open the **Styles and Formatting** task pane.

2 Select a word that is formatted like the text you want to select.

3 Click **Select All**.

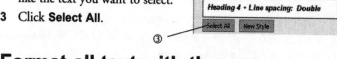

③

Format all text with the same formatting

1 Select all text using the method described above.

2 Pick a new formatting style from the list, or click **New Style** to create a new formatting style.

②

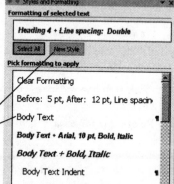

Set up AutoFormat

Word can format your document automatically. There are a number of AutoFormat options that you can set up.

1 In the **Tools** menu, select **AutoCorrect Options**.

2 Click on the **AutoFormat** tab.

3 Select appropriate AutoFormat options.

4 Click **OK**.

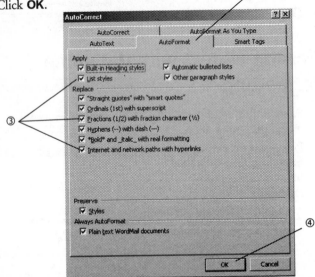

Apply AutoFormat to the whole document

1 In the **Format** menu, select **AutoFormat**.

2 To be safe, select **AutoFormat and review each change**.

3 Select a document type and click **OK**.

4 Scroll through the formatted document to see how it looks.

5 Once formatting is completed, review the changes as follows:

- To undo all formatting changes, select **Reject All**.
- To accept all formatting changes, select **Accept All**.
- To consider each change individually, select **Review Changes**.

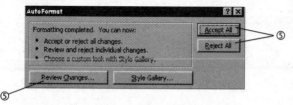

Apply AutoFormat to part of a document

1 Highlight the text that you want to AutoFormat.

2 Repeat steps 1–5 on previous page.

Review AutoFormat changes

You can keep some AutoFormat changes and reject others:

1 Click **Review Changes** at the end of the AutoFormat procedure.

2 A dialog box appears summarizing each change in turn, with the relevant change marked out in red as shown below.

3 For each change choose either **Reject**, or **Find** to accept it and move to the next one.

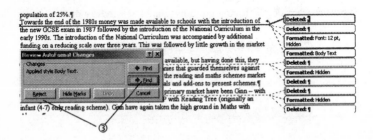

Format a document automatically as you type

1 In the **Tools** menu, select **AutoCorrect Options**.

2 Click on the **AutoFormat As You Type** tab.

3 Select from the AutoFormat options available.

4 Click **OK**.

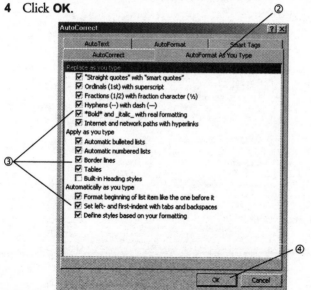

Turn on Click and Type

Click and Type is a feature in Word that allows you to type text anywhere on a page, not just at the start of a line.

1 In the **Tools** menu, select **Options**.

2 Click on the **Edit** tab.

3 Tick the **Enable Click and Type** check box.

4 Click **OK**.

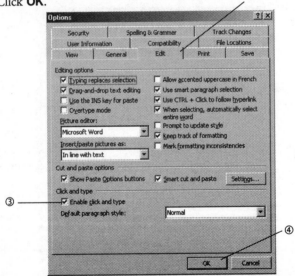

Use Click and Type

1 Switch to **Print Layout View** or **Web Layout View**.

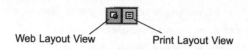

Web Layout View   Print Layout View

2 Move the cursor to a blank area where you want to insert text or a graphic.

3 Click to activate the **Click and Type** pointer.

4 Double-click, and then start typing.

Change the case of text

1 Highlight the text whose case you want to change.

2 In the **Format** menu, select **Change Case**.

3 Make an appropriate selection.

4 Click **OK**.

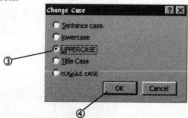

Keep lines or paragraphs together on a page

1 Select the lines or paragraphs that you want to keep together.
2 In the **Format** menu, select **Paragraph**.
3 Click on the **Line and Page Breaks** tab.
4 Select **Keep lines together** or **Keep with next** (paragraph).
5 Click **OK**.

Insert a dropped capital

1 Click to the right of the capital letter that you want to drop.

2 In the **Format** menu, select **Drop Cap**.

3 Select the position of the dropped capital.

4 Select any of the other options available.

5 Click **OK**.

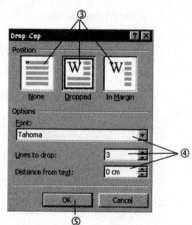

Example of a paragraph
with a dropped capital

When we fed this piece of analysis back to the client, initially he rejected it. We then explored the question, "if we take the proposition as true, does your behaviour make sense?" He agreed with this in a thoughtful way.
We then searched for any other basis, which would completely explain his behaviour. We found none.

Insert symbols and special characters

1 Move cursor to where you want to insert the symbol or special character.

2 In the **Insert** menu, select **Symbol**.

3 Click on the **Symbols** tab.

4 Choose an appropriate font.

5 Click on the character that you want to use.

6 Click **Insert**.

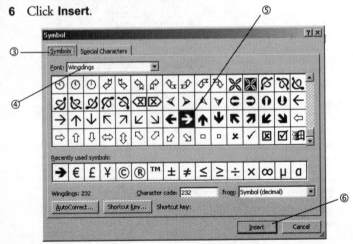

Switch between imperial and metric measurement

You can change the default unit that Word uses for measurements.

1 In the **Tools** menu, select **Options**.

2 Click on the **General** tab.

3 In the **Measurement units** box, click to select the unit that you want to use.

4 Click **OK**.

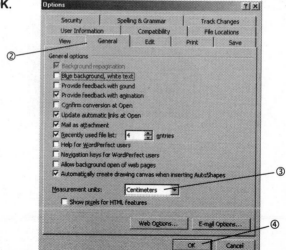

Hyphenate words automatically

Word can hyphenate words automatically to make lines in a paragraph of text more even.

1 In the **Tools** menu, point to **Language** and select **Hyphenation**.

2 Click to select **Automatically hyphenate document**.

3 Make other changes to hyphenation settings as appropriate.

4 Click **OK**.

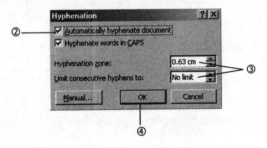

Hyphenate words manually

1 In the **Tools** menu, point to **Language** and select **Hyphenation**.
2 Set an appropriate hyphenation zone.
3 Limit the number of consecutive hyphens as appropriate.
4 Click **Manual**.

Word will display each proposed hyphen in turn:

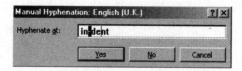

- Click **Yes** to accept the proposed hyphen.
- Click **No** to reject the proposed hyphen.
- Click at a new point inside the word to hyphenate it differently.

Set widows and orphans control

Sometimes a single line from a paragraph ends up on its own on the next page. Widow/orphan control can stop this from happening.

1   Highlight the paragraph.
2   In the **Format** menu, select **Paragraph**.
3   Click to select the **Line and Page Breaks** tab.
4   Click to select **Widow/Orphan control**.
5   Click **OK**.

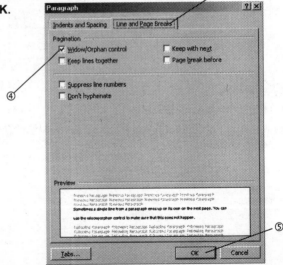

View Format settings for a paragraph

1 In the **Help** menu, select **What's This?**

2 Click the text whose formatting you want to view.

3 A comprehensive **Reveal Formatting** information box appears.

tip

You can keep the **Reveal Formatting** pane open, to monitor the formatting you are using, and to compare the formatting of several words, sentences or paragraphs.

Reveal Formatting ▾ ✕

Selected text

Sample Text

☐ Compare to another selection

Formatting of selected text

⊟ **Font**
Font:
 (Default) Tahoma
 11 pt
Language:
 English (U.K.)

⊟ **Paragraph**
Alignment:
 Left
Indentation:
 Left: 0.63 cm
 Hanging: 0.63 cm
 Right: 0 cm
Spacing:
 Line spacing: Double
Tabs:
 Tabs: 1.27 cm, List tab

⊟ **Bullets and Numbering**
List:
 Numbered
 Level: 1
 Numbering Style: 1, 2, 3, ...
 Start at: 1
 Alignment: Left
 Aligned at: 0.63 cm
 Tab after: 1.27 cm
 Indent at: 1.27 cm

Options

☐ Distinguish style source
☐ Show all formatting marks

Convert text to a bulleted or numbered list

1 Highlight the text that you want to be bulleted or numbered.

2 Click on the appropriate icon in the Formatting toolbar.

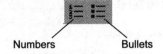

Numbers   Bullets

Create a list as you type

1 Move cursor to the point where you want a bulleted or numbered list.

2 Click on the appropriate icon in the Formatting toolbar.

3 Begin typing.

4 Create the next bulleted or numbered point by pressing **[Enter]**.

Add to a bulleted or numbered list

1 Click at the end of the last line of the list.

2 Press **[Enter]**.

3 A new bullet or numbered point will appear automatically.

Convert bullets to numbers

1 Highlight the bulleted list.

2 Click on the **Numbers** icon.

Undo a bulleted or numbered list

1 Highlight the bulleted or numbered list.

2 Click on the appropriate icon ▤ ▤ in the Formatting toolbar.

Or

1 In the **Format** menu, select **Bullets and Numbering**.

2 Select **None**.

3 Click **OK**.

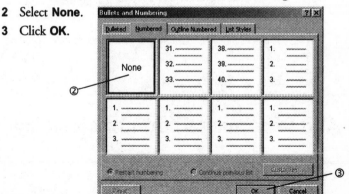

Customize bullets and numbers

1 Highlight the numbered or bulleted list.
2 In the **Format** menu, select **Bullets and Numbering**.
3 Select an appropriate number or bullet style.
4 Click Customize... for further options.

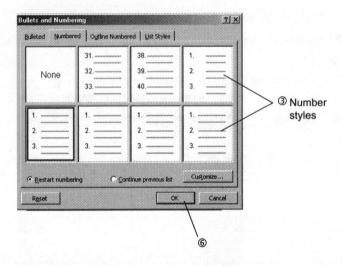

③ Number styles

⑥

5 Click **OK**.

6 Click **OK**.

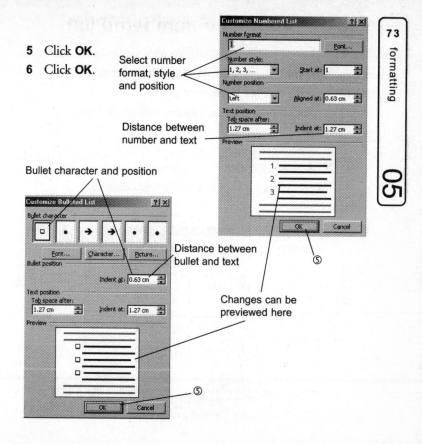

Select number
format, style
and position

Distance between
number and text

Bullet character and position

Distance between
bullet and text

Changes can be
previewed here

Create an outline numbered list

You can create an outline numbered list with up to nine levels.

1 In the **Format** menu, select **Bullets and Numbering**.
2 Click on the **Outline Numbered** tab.
3 Click to select an appropriate outline numbering format.
4 Click **OK**.
5 Type your numbered list.

   • To demote a list item to a lower numbering level, click ⬛.
   • To promote a list item to a higher level, click ⬛.

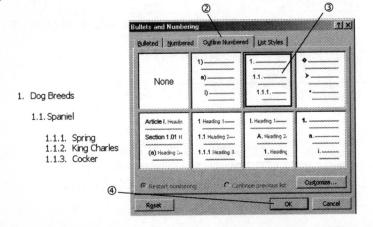

1. Dog Breeds

   1.1. Spaniel

      1.1.1. Spring
      1.1.2. King Charles
      1.1.3. Cocker

Use a style

A style is a collection of formatting characteristics that has been given a name. Applying a style enables you to make several formatting changes in one go.

There are two kinds of styles:

- Paragraph styles apply to whole paragraphs. They specify a combination of font, indentation, line spacing, tabs etc.
- Character styles define the look of one or more characters, and specify formatting such as font, underlining and bold.

Word comes with several predefined styles, or you can create your own.

Create a new style

1 In the **Format** menu, select **Styles and Formatting**.

2 Select **New Style**.

3 Give the style a name.

4 Select a **Style type**.

5 Place a tick in the **Add to template** check box.

6 Click the **Format** button and select **Font**.

7 Select a font style and size and Click **OK**.

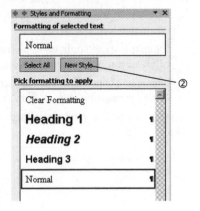

8 Click again on the format button and repeat steps 6 and 7 for each of the remaining options that are applicable.

9 Click **OK**.

10 Click **OK**.

You will now be able to select the style you have created in the **Style name** drop-down list.

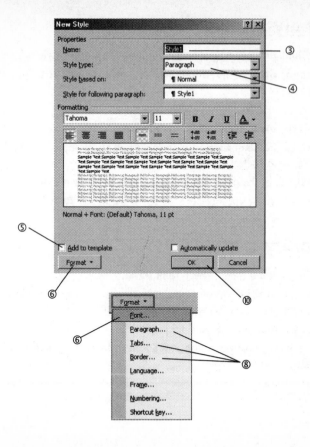

Apply a style

1 Highlight the paragraph that you want to apply a style to.
2 In the **Style name** drop-down list, select the style that you want to apply.

Or

1 In the **View** menu, select **Task Pane**.
2 Click on the downward-pointing arrow at the top of the **Task Pane** and select **Styles and Formatting**.
3 Highlight the paragraph that you want to apply a style to.
4 Click on the appropriate style displayed in the **Task Pane**.

Modify a style

1 In the **View** menu, select **Task Pane**.
2 Click on the downward-pointing arrow at the top of the **Task Pane** and select **Styles and Formatting**.
3 Right-click the style and select **Modify**.
4 Make any changes to the Style's font or formatting, and select **OK** after each change.

The most commonly used formatting
options can be set from the toolbar

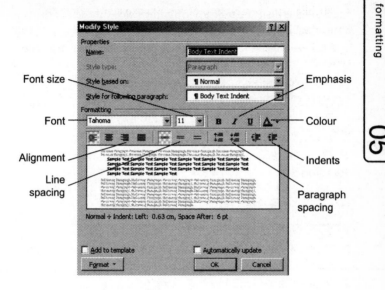

View style names

The current style name is displayed in the field at the left of the Formatting Toolbar. The default style name is normal.

1 Click on downward point arrow to right of the **Style Name** to see the list of style names to choose from.

2 Select **More** to see further **Style** options. They will be displayed in the Task Pane.

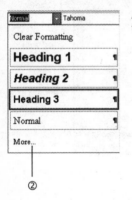

A limited set of Styles are listed in the Formatting toolbar

For advanced work on Styles, use the Task Pane

06

margins and tabs

Set left/right margins with ruler

1   In the **View** menu, select **Ruler**.

2   Change the display to **Print Layout View**. The shaded parts of the ruler indicate the left and right margins.

3   Move the mouse pointer to the left or right end of the white part of the ruler. The mouse pointer will change into a twin-headed arrow.

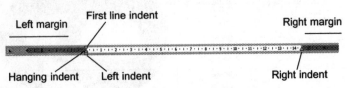

Left margin   First line indent   Right margin

Hanging indent   Left indent   Right indent

4   Click and drag the margin to the desired position.

5   Release the mouse.

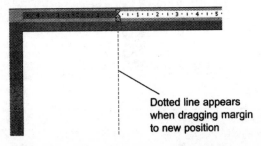

Dotted line appears when dragging margin to new position

Set top/bottom margin using ruler

1 In the **View** menu, select **Ruler**.

2 Change the display to **Print Layout View**. The shaded parts of the ruler on the left-hand side of the screen indicate the top and bottom margins.

3 Move the mouse pointer to the top or bottom end of the white part of the ruler. The mouse pointer will change into a twin-headed arrow.

4 Click and drag the margin to the desired position.

5 Release the mouse.

Top margin

Set margins using a dialog box

1 In the **File** menu, select **Page Setup**.
2 Click on the **Margins** tab.
3 Enter values for top, bottom, left or right margins.
4 Click **OK**.

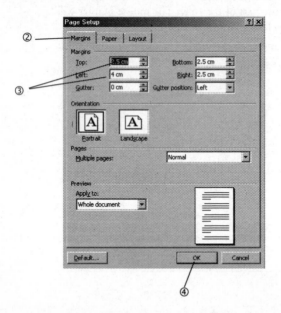

Create a hanging indent

A hanging indent is when all the lines in a paragraph are indented apart from the first one.

1 In the **View** menu, select **Ruler**.

2 Change the display to **Print Layout View**.

3 Click anywhere inside the paragraph in which you want to add a hanging indent.

4 Click on the hanging indent marker and drag to the desired position.

5 Release the mouse.

Drag into position

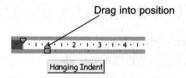

Hanging Indent

Indent the first line of a paragraph

1   In the **View** menu, select **Ruler**.

2   Change the display to **Print Layout View**.

3   Click anywhere inside the paragraph in which you want a first
    line indent.

4   Click on the first line indent marker and drag to the desired
    position.

5   Release the mouse.

Drag into position

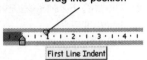

First Line Indent

Indent all the lines of a paragraph

1   In the **View** menu, select **Ruler**.

2   Change the display to **Print Layout View**.

3   Click anywhere inside the paragraph that you want to indent.

4   Click on the left indent marker and drag to the desired position.

5   Release the mouse.

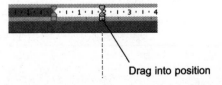

Drag into position

Indent lines using the menu

1 Highlight the text that you want to indent.
2 In the **Format** menu, select **Paragraph**.
3 Click on **Indents and Spacing** tab.
4 Enter desired indent values.
5 Click **OK**.

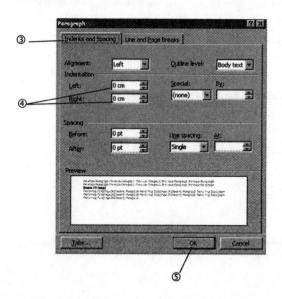

Indent right-hand edge of paragraph

1 In the **View** menu, select **Ruler**.
2 Change the display to **Print Layout View**.
3 Click anywhere inside the paragraph that you want to indent.
4 Click on the right indent marker and drag to the desired position.
5 Release the mouse.

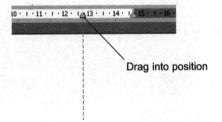

Drag into position

Change default tab stops

By default, Word has tab stops set at intervals of 1.27cm (about half an inch). Every time you press [**Tab**] the cursor moves 1.27 cm to the next tab stop.

You can change the default tab stop settings.

1 In the **Format** menu, select **Tabs**.
2 Enter a new value in the **Default tab stops** field.
3 Click **OK**.

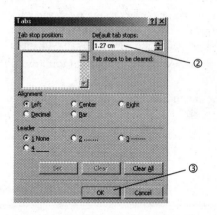

Use custom tab stops

Tabs help you to control the alignment of text in a document.
There are four main types of tab stops.

Left tab   Centre tab   Right tab   Decimal tab

1 Click the tab symbol until you see the tab that you want.
2 Move the mouse pointer to the ruler, and click and hold where
  you want the tab. A vertical line will appear through your
  document, indicating where the tab will appear.
3 Drag the mouse to the left or right until the tab is in the desired
  position.
4 Release the mouse.

Move a custom tab stop

1 Move the cursor over the tab stop symbol in the ruler.
2 Click and drag the tab stop to its new position.
3 Release the mouse.

Delete a custom tab stop

1 Move the cursor over the tab stop symbol in the ruler.
2 Click and drag the symbol away from the ruler.
3 Release the mouse.

Line up rows of figures by their decimal point

1 Highlight the rows of figures to line up.
2 Click on the tab symbol until ▦ appears.
3 Place tab stop at appropriate place in the ruler.
4 Click at start of each row of figures.
5 Press **[Tab]** once.

12.25
13.05
2.95
245.95

12.25
13.05
2.95
245.95

Before placing decimal tab stop, figures are not aligned

With decimal tab stop in place, rows of figures are aligned properly

Set precise measurements for tabs

1 In the **Format** menu, select **Tabs**.
2 Enter a value in **Tab stop position** field.
3 Select the appropriate alignment.
4 Click **OK**.

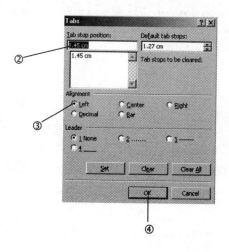

Set tab stops with leader characters

1 Highlight the paragraph in which you want tab stops with leader characters.

2 In the **Format** menu, select **Tabs**.

3 In the **Tab stop position** field, enter a value for a new tab or select an existing one.

4 Click the desired leader type.

5 Click **Set**.

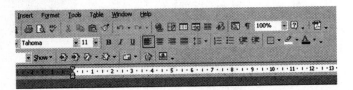

Tab stop with leader characters

Beans on toast..£2.40
Mushrooms on toast...£2.75
Scrambled egg on toast...£2.50
Poached egg on toast £2.50

07

headers and footers

Add page numbers

Word can automatically number the pages of your document.

1 In the **Insert** menu, select **Page Numbers**.

2 Select where the numbers should be positioned, and how they should be aligned.

3 Click on **Format** to see other page numbering options.

4 Click **OK**.

5 Click **OK**.

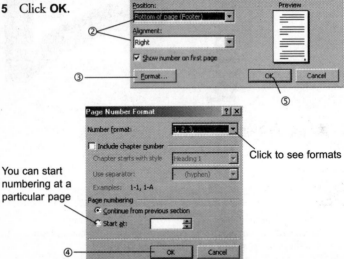

You can start numbering at a particular page

Click to see formats

Add a header (running head)

1 In the **View** menu, select **Header and Footer**.
2 Type an appropriate running head where indicated.
3 Highlight the running head and apply any formatting (e.g. font settings) you require.
4 Click **Close**.

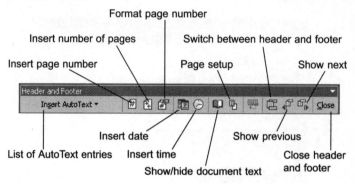

Format page number

Insert number of pages

Insert page number

Page setup

Switch between header and footer

Show next

List of AutoText entries   Insert date   Insert time

Show previous

Show/hide document text

Close header and footer

tip

AutoText entries, such as page numbers, are automatically updated as your document changes, and so are always more efficient than manual entries.

Add a footer

1 In the **View** menu, select **Header and Footer**.

2 Click on 🔲 to move the cursor from header to footer area.

3 Type appropriate footer text, or select an appropriate AutoText entry.

4 Click **Close**.

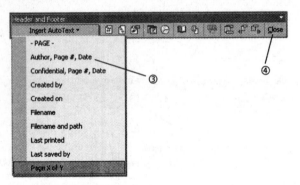

Remove a header or footer

1 In the **View** menu, select **Header and Footer**.

2 Select the text in the header or footer that you want to remove.

3 Press **[Del]**.

Specify different headers and footers

Often you want a different running head on odd and even pages.

1 In the **File** menu, select **Page Setup**.

2 Click on the **Layout** tab.

3 Below **Headers and footers**, place a tick in **Different odd and even**.

4 Tick **Different first page** if the first page of your document will have its own header/ footer.

5 Click **OK**.

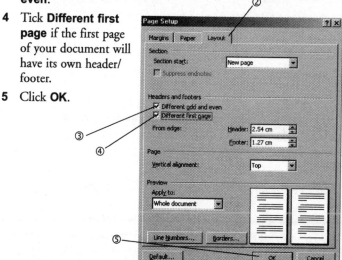

Specify first page header or footer

1 Follow the instructions to **Specify different headers and footers**.

2 Move the cursor to the start of the document.

3 In the **View** menu, select **Header and Footer**.

4 Enter the first page **Header** text.

5 Click on  to move the cursor to the first page footer.

6 Enter the first page **Footer** text.

7 Click **Close**.

First Page Header

Header and Footer
Insert AutoText ▾   Close

Specify even page header or footer

1 Follow instructions to **Specify different headers and footers**.

2 Move the cursor to the first even page of the document.

3 In the **View** menu, select **Header and Footer**.

4 Enter the even page **Header** text.

5 Click on  to move the cursor to the even page footer.

6 Enter the even page **Footer** text.

7 Click **Close**.

Even Page Header

Specify odd page header or footer

1 Follow the instructions to **Specify different headers and footers**.

2 Move the cursor to the first odd page of the document.

3 In the **View** menu, select **Header and Footer**.

4 Enter the odd page **Header** text.

5 Click on  to move the cursor to the odd page footer.

6 Enter the odd page **Footer** text.

7 Click **Close**.

Add a footnote

1 Move cursor to where you want the footnote mark to appear.
2 In the **Insert** menu, point to **Reference** and select **Footnote**.
3 Select **Footnotes**.
4 Select the **Location** from the drop-down menu.
5 Choose a number format.
6 Click **Insert**.

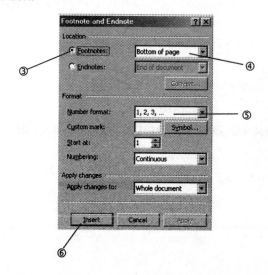

7 Type the text to appear in the footnote.

8 Highlight the footnote text, right-click on it, and select **Go to Footnote** to return to that point in the document.

> In the echo chamber
> of my mind,
> your voice still whispers[1]
> lyrics of a sweeter,
> more lovely song.
>
> (29/8/98)

---

[1] Compare with Flicker Flame (Sept 97)

Example of a footnote

Delete a footnote or endnote

1 Highlight the footnote or endnote marker.

2 Press **[Del]**.

Add an endnote

An endnote is identical to a footnote, except that all the notes appear at the end of the document, rather than on each page.

1 Move the cursor to where you want the endnote mark.

2 In the **Insert** menu, point to **Reference** and select **Footnote**.

3 Select **Endnotes**.

4 Select the **Location** from the drop-down menu.

5 Choose a numbering format.

6 Click **Insert**.

7 Type the text to appear in the endnote.

8 Highlight the note text, right-click on it, and select **Go to Footnote** to return to that point in the document.

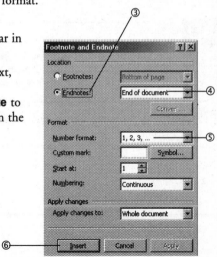

Edit a footnote or endnote

1 Move the cursor over the footnote marker within the text.

2 Double-click to move the cursor straight to the footnote or endnote text.

3 Make the appropriate corrections.

4 Highlight the revised text, right-click, and select **Go to Footnote**. This will move the cursor back to the footnote mark.

tip

If you have ScreenTips switched on (see page 239), the footnote text may appear in a caption bubble whenever you move your mouse over a footnote or endnote marker.

Insert a cross-reference

1 Type the text that is to accompany the cross-reference.

   (e.g. *For further information, see Page X*).

2 In the **Insert** menu, point to **Reference** and select **Cross-reference**.

3 Select the appropriate **Reference type**.

4 Select an appropriate reference insertion point.

5 Click to select the cross-reference.

6 Click **Insert**.

7 Click **Close**.

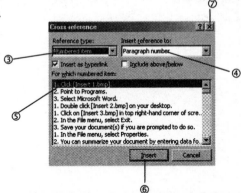

Insert a hyperlink cross-reference

1 Type the text that is to accompany the cross-reference.
2 In the **Insert** menu, point to **Reference** and select **Cross-reference**.
3 Select the appropriate **Reference type**.
4 Select an appropriate reference insertion point.
5 Click to select the cross-reference.
6 Click to select **Insert as hyperlink**.
7 Click **Insert**.
8 Click **Close**.

08

proofing tools

Check spelling and grammar as you type

1 In the **Tools** menu, select **Options**.

2 Click on the **Spelling & Grammar** tab.

3 Place a tick in **Check spelling as you type**.

4 Place a tick in **Check grammar as you type**.

5 Select any other spelling or grammar options and click **OK**.

From now on, Word will automatically place a wavy red line under words that it does not recognize, and a wavy green line under common grammatical errors.

Correct spelling or grammar

1 Right-click on a wavy red or green line.

2 Select the appropriate correction

Or

3 Select **Ignore All** (to keep the word as it is spelled in the document).

Or

4 Select **Add to Dictionary** (to add the word to the computer's dictionary).

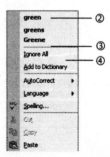

Correct spelling and grammar in a complete document

1 Click ![spell check icon].

Or

In the **Tools** menu, select **Spelling and Grammar**.

2 Select an appropriate response to each error found.

3 Click **Close** when the spelling check is complete.

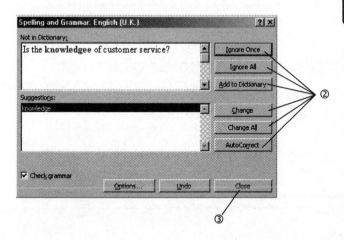

Set spelling and grammar options

1 In the **Tools** menu, select **Options**.
2 Click on the **Spelling & Grammar** tab.
3 Select the appropriate spelling and grammar options.
4 Click **OK**.

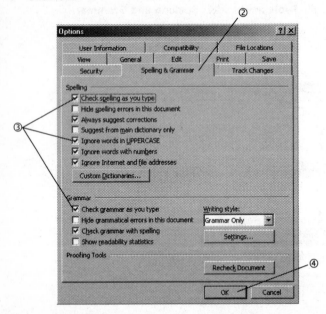

Use AutoCorrect

As its name implies, the AutoCorrect feature automatically corrects common typos and spelling mistakes as you type.

1 In the **Tools** menu, select **AutoCorrect Options**.
2 The correction rules are displayed in the drop-down list.
3 Click **Exceptions** to view or add AutoCorrect exceptions.
4 Click **OK**.

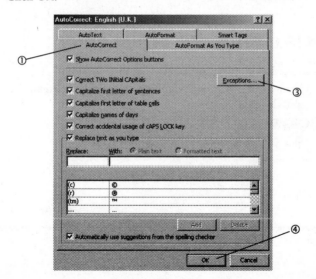

Add an AutoCorrect entry

1 In the **Tools** menu, select **AutoCorrect Options**.
2 Type the symbol or misspelled word in the left-hand column.
3 Type the replacement symbol or text in the right-hand column.
4 Click **Add**.
5 Click **OK**.

Delete an AutoCorrect entry

1 In the **Tools** menu, select **AutoCorrect Options**.
2 Locate the AutoCorrect entry that you want to delete in the scroll-down list.
3 Click **Delete**.
4 Click **OK**.

Use the Thesaurus

1 Right-click on the word that you want to replace.

2 Point to **Synonyms**, and select an alternative word.

Or

3 Select **Thesaurus**.

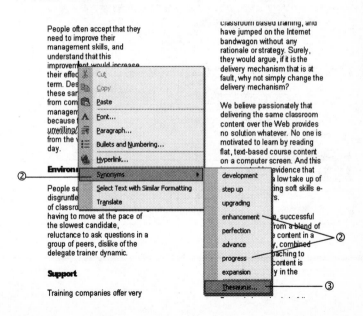

4 Select one of the meanings listed.
5 Select a suitable synonym.
6 Click **Replace**.

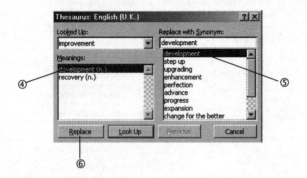

tip

To see more word choices, highlight a synonym and click
Lookup.

Create AutoText entry

If you often find yourself typing the same words and phrases, you can store them as AutoText entries in Word. The next time you start to type the word or phrase, Word will complete it for you.

1 Enter the word or phrase into a document.
2 Highlight it.
3 In the **Insert** menu, point to **AutoText** and select **New**.
4 Word will suggest a name for the AutoText entry, or you can add a name of your own.
5 Click **OK**.

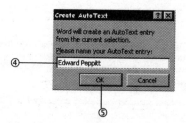

tip

You can save a lot of time if you create **AutoText** entries for contact or place names that you type regularly.

Use an AutoText entry

1 In your document, start to type the AutoText name.
2 As you type, the AutoComplete tip box appears with the full AutoText name.
3 Press **[Enter]**.

If the AutoComplete tip box does not appear, you may find that this feature is switched off. In the **Insert** menu, point to **AutoText** and select **AutoText**. Tick the **Show AutoComplete suggestions** check box.

Switch off proofing for a specific section of text

1 Highlight the text that you do not want to be proofed.
2 In the **Tools** menu, point to **Language** and select **Set Language**.
3 Click to select **Do not check spelling or grammar**.
4 Click **OK**.

Create a new dictionary

You may wish to store technical terms, as well as other specific words or phrases that you use, in your own custom dictionary.

1 In the **Tools** menu, select **Options**.

2 Click to select the **Spelling & Grammar** tab.

3 Click **Dictionaries**.

4 Click **New**.

5 Give the new dictionary a name and click **Save**.

6 Click **OK**.

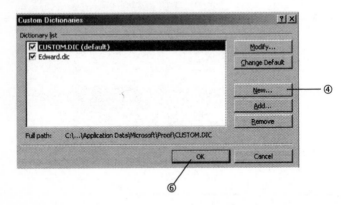

Count the number of words in a document

1 In the **Tools** menu, select **Word Count**.
2 The word count for the complete document will be displayed.
3 Click **Show Toolbar** if you want to repeat your word count periodically as you make revisions to your document.
4 Click **Recount** at any time.
5 Click **OK**.

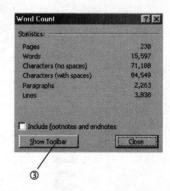

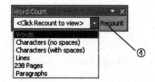

09

tables and columns

Create a simple table

1 Move the cursor to the point in your document where you want a table.

2 In the **Table** menu, point to **Insert**, and select **Table**.

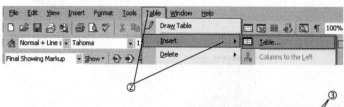

3 Enter the number of columns and rows that you need.

4 Click **OK**.

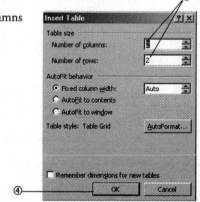

Convert text to a table

1 Insert separator characters (e.g. commas) into the text to indicate where columns should be placed.

2 Highlight the text that you want to convert.

3 In the **Table** menu, point to **Convert** and select **Text to Table**.

4 Select the appropriate separator character where indicated.

5 Click **OK**.

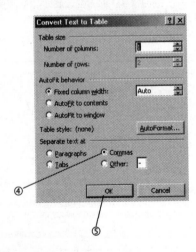

Draw a table

1 In the **Table** menu, select **Draw Table**.

Or

Click ⊞ on the Formatting toolbar.

2 Click ✐.

3 Click and drag the pencil icon across the page until table outline is the right size, and release the mouse.

4 Add columns and rows inside the table outline using the same drawing tool. Draw vertical lines to create columns, and horizontal lines to create rows.

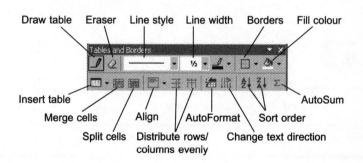

Draw table   Eraser   Line style   Line width   Borders   Fill colour

Insert table

Merge cells   Align   AutoFormat   Sort order   AutoSum

Split cells   Distribute rows/   Change text direction
columns evenly

Select a complete table

1 Click on ⊞ in the top left hand corner of the table.

Or

In the **Table** menu, point to **Select** and select **Table**.

	Charlotte	Tim

Click to select
the complete
table

tip

To undo the most recent row or column you have added, click
. To undo any other part of the table, select ⌧ and drag it
over the lines you want to remove.

Select a row

1 Move the cursor to the left of the table until it changes to a
  white arrow pointing to the row that you wish to select.

2 Click once.

Or

1 Click inside the first cell in the row you wish to select.

2 Drag the mouse across all the cells in that row.

Select a column

1 Move the cursor to above the table until it changes to a black
  arrow pointing down to the column you wish to select.

2 Click once.

Or

1 Click inside the first cell in the column you wish to select.

2 Drag the mouse down all the cells in that column.

Sort a column within a table

1 Highlight the column or cells that you want to sort.
2 In the **Table** menu, select **Sort**.
3 Select appropriate sort options.
4 Click **Options**.
5 Select **Sort column only**.
6 Click **OK**.
7 Click **OK**.

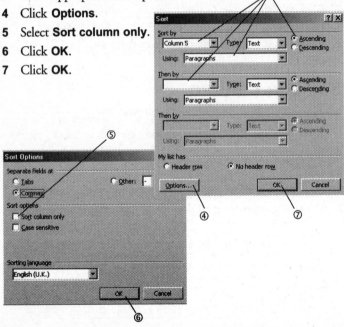

Use Table AutoFormat

1 Click anywhere inside the table.
2 In the **Table** menu, select **Table AutoFormat**.
3 Choose an appropriate table style.
4 Click **Modify** to select other formatting options.
5 Click **OK**.
6 Click **Apply**.

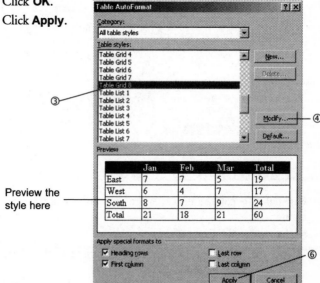

Preview the style here

Table AutoFormat

Category:
All table styles

Table styles:
Table Grid 4
Table Grid 5
Table Grid 6
Table Grid 7
Table Grid 8
Table List 1
Table List 2
Table List 3
Table List 4
Table List 5
Table List 6
Table List 7

New...
Delete...
Modify...
Default...

Preview

	Jan	Feb	Mar	Total
East	7	7	5	19
West	6	4	7	17
South	8	7	9	24
Total	21	18	21	60

Apply special formats to
☑ Heading rows   ☐ Last row
☑ First column   ☐ Last column

Apply   Cancel

Add rows to a table

1 Highlight the row above or below where you wish to add a new row.

2 In the **Table** menu, point to **Insert**.

3 Select either **Rows Above** or **Rows Below**.

Add columns to a table

1 Highlight the column next to where you wish to add a new column.

2 In the **Table** menu, point to **Insert**.

3 Select either **Columns to the left** or **Columns to the right**.

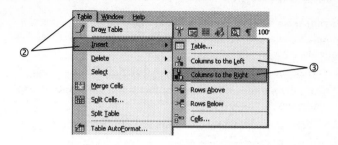

Insert a tab into a table

If you press [**Tab**] inside a table, the cursor moves automatically to the next cell. Sometimes, however, you need to place a tab within a cell.

1 Click inside the table cell.

2 Hold down [**Ctrl**] and press [**Tab**].

You will need to insert tabs inside the cells of a table if you want to line up a column of numbers or figures.

Add up figures in a table column

If your table contains figures and other data, you can perform simple calculations without the need to incorporate an Excel spreadsheet.

1 Select the table containing figures that you want to add up.

2 In the **View** menu, point to **Toolbars** and select **Tables and Borders**.

3 Click inside the empty cell at the end of the column of figures.

4 Click the **AutoSum** button.

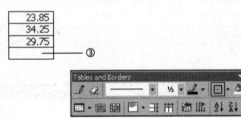

Add up figures in a table row

1 Select the table containing figures that you want to add up.
2 In the **View** menu, point to **Toolbars** and select **Tables and Borders**.
3 Click inside the empty cell at the end of the row of figures.
4 Click the **AutoSum** button.

Update calculations in a table

If you make changes to the figures in a table, the totals will not recalculate automatically like in a full Excel spreadsheet.

To update calculations:

1 Select the table.
2 Press **[F9]**.

Put text into columns

Columns are an alternative to tables for laying text in several blocks on a page.

1 Highlight the text that you want to put into columns.

2 Click ▦ .

3 Drag mouse across the number of columns that you want.

4 Click the mouse.

Revert to a single column

1 Highlight the text in columns.

2 Click ▦ .

3 Drag the mouse across to a single column.

4 Click the mouse button.

Alter the column layout

1 Click in any part of the document with columns.
2 In the **Format** menu, select **Columns**.
3 Change the number, width and spacing of columns.
4 Click **OK**.

③ Number of columns

③ Width and spacing

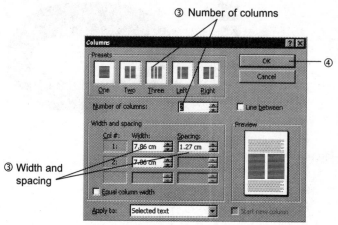

10

graphics

Display picture toolbar

The Picture toolbar contains all the tools you are likely to need to insert and edit pictures and simple graphics.

1 In the **View** menu, point to **Toolbars** and select **Picture**.

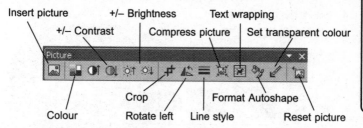

Insert picture +/– Brightness Text wrapping
+/– Contrast Compress picture Set transparent colour
Crop Format Autoshape
Colour Rotate left Line style Reset picture

Display drawing toolbar

The Drawing toolbar contains all the tools you are likely to need to draw and amend common shapes and lines.

1 In the **View** menu, point to **Toolbars** and select **Drawing**.

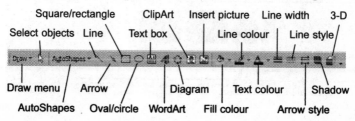

Square/rectangle ClipArt Insert picture Line width 3-D
Select objects Line Text box Line colour Line style
Draw menu Arrow Line style
AutoShapes Oval/circle WordArt Diagram Fill colour Text colour Arrow style Shadow

Insert a picture into a document

1 Move the cursor to where you want to insert the picture.

2 In the **Insert** menu, point to **Picture** and select **From File**.

3 Navigate to the drive or folder where the picture file is stored.

4 Select the picture file.

5 Click **Insert**.

Edit a picture within a document

1 Click on the picture/graphic to select it. A frame with eight black sizing handles will appear around the picture.

2 Click and drag one of the black sizing handles to resize the picture.

3 Right-click and select **Format Picture** to make changes to other properties of the picture.

4 Click **OK** when finished.

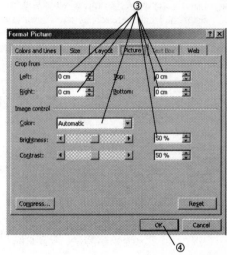

tip

To maintain the picture's proportion, click and drag on a corner sizing handle.

Insert Clip Art

1 Move the cursor to where you want to insert Clip Art.

2 In the **Insert** menu, point to **Picture** and select **Clip Art**. The **Task Pane** will be displayed.

3 Enter a keyword describing what you are looking for, and click **Search**. Images matching the search criteria will be displayed.

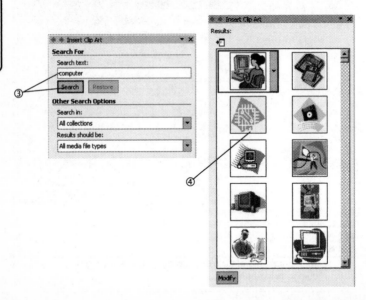

4 Click on the downward-pointing arrow to the right of an image to view the Clip Art shortcut menu.

5 Preview the picture if desired.

6 Click **Insert**.

⑥ — Insert

Copy

✕ Delete from Clip Organizer

Open Clip In...

Tools on the Web...

Copy to Collection...

Move to Collection...

Edit Keywords...

Find Similar Style

Preview/Properties — ⑤

④

Clip Art shortcut menu

If you have the Task Pane displayed, you can reach the Clip Art menu more quickly by using the shortcut menu. Click on the downward-pointing arrow at the top of the Task Pane, and select **Insert Clip Art**.

Crop a picture with mouse

1 Click on the picture to select it.

2 In the **View** menu, point to **Toolbars** and select **Picture**.

3 Click ⊬ on the Picture toolbar.

4 Move the mouse pointer over a sizing handle.

5 Click and drag the sizing handle towards the centre of the picture/graphic.

6 Repeat for the other sizing handles as required.

7 Click away from the picture to de-select it.

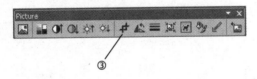

Crop/resize a picture using the Format Picture dialog box

1 Double-click on the picture to open the dialog box.

Or

   Right-click on the picture and select **Format Picture**.

2 Click on the **Picture** tab.

3 Enter the crop values.

4 Click on **Size** tab.

5 Enter the size values.

6 Click **OK**.

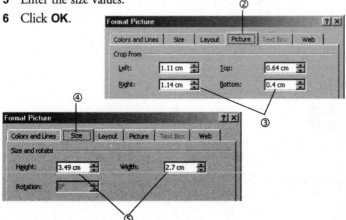

Resize a picture

1 Click the picture to select it.
2 Move the mouse pointer to a sizing handle.
3 Click and drag the sizing handle until the image is the desired size.

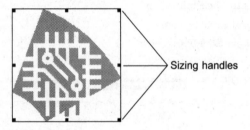

Sizing handles

To keep the resized image in proportion, click and drag a corner sizing handle only.

Adjust contrast/brightness of picture

1 Click the picture to select it.
2 In the **View** menu, point to **Toolbars** and select **Picture**.
3 Click on the appropriate button on the Picture Toolbar.

Increase contrast   Decrease contrast

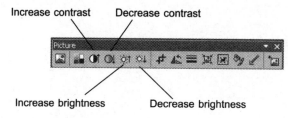

Increase brightness   Decrease brightness

You may find that a colour Clip Art file prints better on a black and white printer if you adjust the contrast and brightness first.

Wrap text around a picture

1 Display the Picture Toolbar.

2 Click the picture to select it.

3 Click the **Text Wrap** button on the Picture Toolbar.

4 Choose a text wrap option from the drop-down menu.

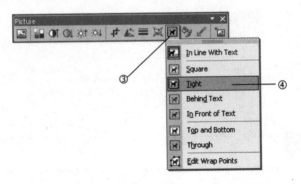

Keep picture in line with text

1 Click the picture to select it.
2 In the **Format** menu, select **Picture**.
3 Click on the **Layout** tab.
4 Click **In line with text**.
5 Click **OK**.

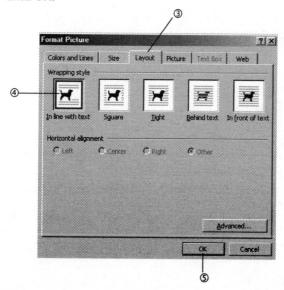

Copy a picture

1 Click the picture to select it.

2 Click .

3 Move the cursor to where you want to copy the picture to.

4 Click .

Move a picture

1 Click the picture to select it.
2 Click and drag to its new location.
3 Release the mouse button.

tip

If you have chosen to keep your picture in line with text, you
will only be able to move it to the start of a new line. If you
have chosen a different text wrapping option, you will be able
to move the picture to any point in your document.

Group drawing objects

If you have two or more pictures together on a page, you may wish to group them together, so that if you move one picture, the other moves with it.

1 Hold down **[Shift]** and select the objects that you want to group together.

2 On the Drawing toolbar, click **Draw** and select **Group**.

Ungroup objects

1 Click to select the grouped objects.

2 On the Drawing toolbar, click **Draw** and select **Ungroup**.

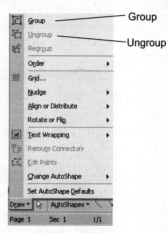

Group

Ungroup

You can also keep drawing objects together using the drawing canvas. See page 157.

Fix the position of a picture

1 Right-click on the picture, and select **Format Picture**.
2 Click on the **Layout** tab.
3 Click on the **Advanced** tab.
4 Click on the **Picture Position** tab.

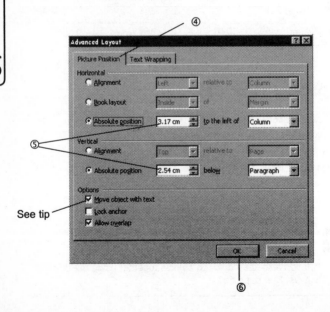

See tip

5 Enter values for the vertical and horizontal anchors.

6 Click **OK**.

tip

You can fix a picture to a paragraph so that the two move together. Select the **Move object with text** check box to ensure that the picture moves up or down with the paragraph it is anchored to. Select the **Lock anchor** check box to ensure that the picture remains anchored to the same paragraph when you move it.

Insert AutoShapes

1 Display the Drawing toolbar.

2 Click **AutoShapes** on the Drawing toolbar to see the common shapes you can draw automatically.

3 Click on an AutoShape to select it.

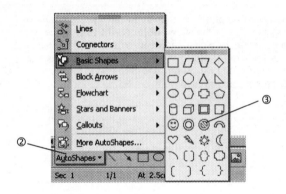

4 The shape will be drawn inside a drawing canvas (see page 157).

5 Click and drag the mouse to create the shape in your document.

6 Release the mouse.

7 Click the shape to select it, and format it using the tools on the drawing toolbar.

8 When you are happy with the shape, use the sizing handles around the drawing canvas to shrink the canvas so that it fits snugly around the shape.

You can delete the drawing canvas altogether:

1 Drag the AutoShape away from the drawing canvas.

2 Click to select the drawing canvas.

3 Press **[Del]**.

To keep the dimensions of the shape in proportion, hold down **[Shift]** while clicking and dragging the mouse.

Draw/edit lines

1 Display the Drawing toolbar.

2 Click 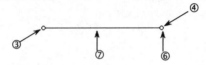 to select it.

3 Move the mouse pointer to where you want to draw a line.

4 Click and drag the mouse to draw the line.

5 Release the mouse.

   • The shape will be drawn inside a drawing canvas (see page 157).

6 Click on one of the sizing handles to resize the line.

7 Click and drag on the line to move it.

8 Right-click on the line and select **Format AutoShape**.

9 Amend the line weight and style, colour and size.

10 Click **OK** when finished.

11 When you are happy with the line, use the sizing handles around the drawing canvas to shrink the canvas so that it fits snugly around the line.

You can delete the drawing canvas altogether (see page 153).

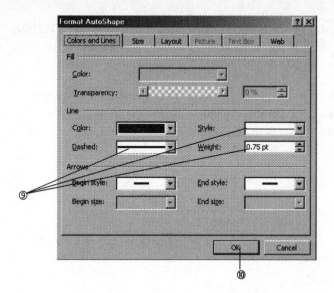

Draw simple ovals and rectangles

1 Display the Drawing toolbar.
2 Click on ▢ or ◯.
3 Move the pointer to where you want to draw your shape.
4 Click and drag the mouse to draw the shape.
5 The shape will be drawn inside a drawing canvas.

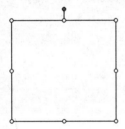

6 If you want to draw either a circle or a square, hold down
   [Shift] while clicking and dragging.
7 When you are happy with the shape, use the sizing handles
   around the drawing canvas to shrink the canvas so that it fits
   snugly around the shape.

Arrange and align graphics using the drawing canvas

You can draw several shapes inside a single drawing canvas, so that they remain grouped together, regardless of the text and other images that flow around them.

1 Draw the first shape as described on page 154.
2 Draw the second shape inside the same drawing canvas.
3 Repeat until the drawing is complete.
4 Right-click on the drawing canvas and select **Format Drawing Canvas**.
5 Amend layout, size and colour as desired.
6 Click **OK**.

Draw common diagrams and diagram shapes

In Word, you can draw common diagram shapes automatically, leaving you just to add captions and any other text and styles that you require.

1 Display the Drawing toolbar (see page 137).

2 Click ⬛.

3 Click to select the diagram type.

4 Click **OK**.

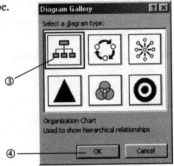

5 Add text where appropriate. Right-click the diagram element and select **Edit Text**.

6 Amend the diagram using the tools in the Diagram toolbar.

7 Click outside the diagram to deselect it when you have finished.

Example of a diagram
before editing

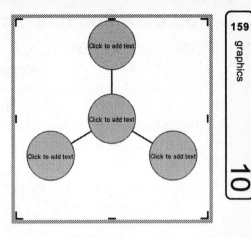

The Diagram toolbar

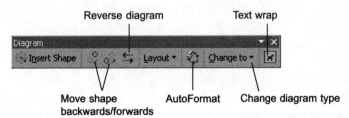

Add a caption to a picture

1 Click to select the picture or graphic.

2 In the **Insert** menu, point to **Reference** and select **Caption**.

3 Select an appropriate Caption **Label**.

4 You can add a new caption label by clicking on **New Label**.

5 Select a position for the caption from the drop-down menu.

6 Enter the caption text.

7 Click **OK**.

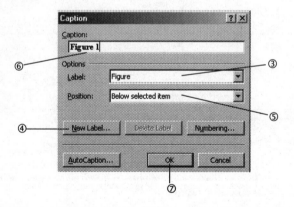

Add captions automatically

1 In the **Insert** menu, point to **Reference** and select **Caption**.

2 Click on **AutoCaption**.

3 Tick to turn on automatic captions for any item in the list.

4 Select an appropriate caption **Label**.

5 You can add a new caption label by clicking on **New Label**.

6 Select a **Position** for the caption from the drop-down list.

• Repeat steps 3–6 to add automatic captions for other items.

7 Click **OK**.

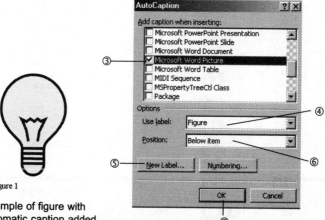

Figure 1

Example of figure with
automatic caption added

11

borders and shading

Add a page border

1 In the **Format** menu, select **Borders and Shading**.
2 Click on the **Page Border** tab.
3 Choose a page border setting.
4 Choose a style, colour and width for your page border.
5 Select the part of your document that you want to display the page border.

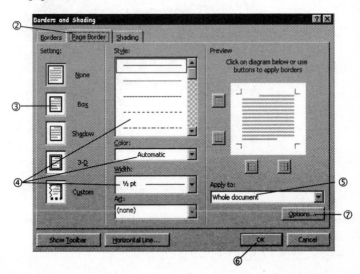

6 Click **OK**.

7 Click **Options** for further customization.

8 Click **OK** when finished.

Adjust the margins
as required

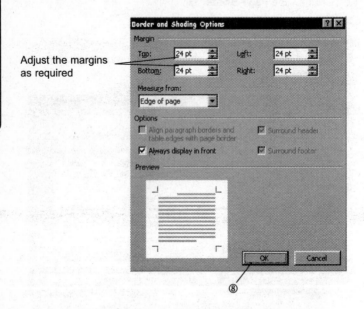

Add an art border

1 In the **Format** menu, select **Borders and Shading**.
2 Click on the **Page Border** tab.

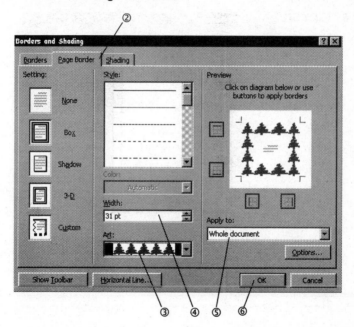

3 Choose an art border from the drop-down list.

4 Select the width of your art border.

5 Select the part of your document that you want to display the art border.

6 Click **OK**.

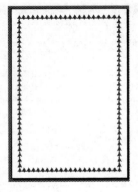

Place a border around text

1 Highlight the text that you want to place a border around.
2 In the **Format** menu, select **Borders and Shading**.
3 Select the border style, colour and width.
4 Click **OK**.

tip

To apply a quick border, click on downward-pointing arrow to the right of the button ▢▾, and select the border that you want to apply.

Place a border around a paragraph

1 Click anywhere inside the paragraph.
2 Click on the downward pointing arrow to the right of the Border button ▢▾.
3 Select the border that you want to apply.

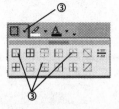

Create a custom border

1 Select the text/paragraph to be given a border.
2 In the **Format** menu, select **Borders and Shading**.
3 Click on the **Borders** tab.
4 Select an appropriate style, colour and width.
5 In the Preview screen, click individual borders to remove them, or re-apply them.
6 Click **OK**.

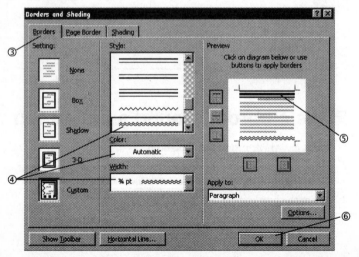

Place a border around an object

1 Right-click on the object and select **Borders and Shading**.
2 Click on the **Borders** tab.
3 Select the border that you want to use.
4 Click **OK**.

You can specify a different style, width and colour for each border line.

Apply shading to text

1 Highlight the text that you want to shade.

2 In the **Format** menu, select **Borders and Shading**.

3 Click on the **Shading** tab.

4 Select the shading colour that you want to use.

5 Click **OK**.

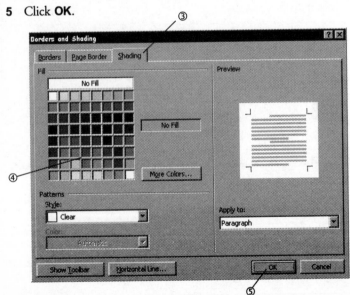

Add a line underneath a paragraph

Sometimes you may want to add a line underneath a paragraph for emphasis.

1 Click on the last line of paragraph.
2 Click on the downward pointing arrow to the right of the Borders button ▣▾.

3 Select .

tip

You can display a Tables and Borders toolbar so that you can add tables, borders and shading more quickly. In the **View** menu, point to **Toolbars** and select **Tables and Borders**.

Change borders

1 Highlight the text/paragraph that contains the border.
2 In the **Format** menu, select **Borders and Shading**.
3 Click on the **Borders** tab.
4 Amend width, style and colour of border.
5 Click **OK**.

Remove borders

1 Highlight the text/paragraph that contains the border.
2 Click on the downward pointing arrow to the right of the Borders button □▾.
3 Click ⬚.

Or

1 Highlight the text/paragraph that contains the border.
2 In the **Format** menu, select **Borders and Shading**.
3 Click **None**.
4 Click **OK**.

12

charts and worksheets

Create a simple chart

Word comes with Microsoft Chart to make drawing a chart really straightforward.

1 In the **Insert** menu, point to **Picture** and select **Chart**.
2 Replace the sample data and headings in the datasheet with your own.

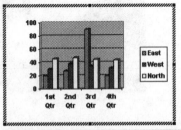

D:\My Documents\Hodder\Com▓▓▓ - Datasheet		A	B	C	D	E
		1st Qtr	2nd Qtr	3rd Qtr	4th Qtr	
1	East	20.4	27.4	90	20.4	
2	West	30.6	38.6	34.6	31.6	
3	North	45.9	46.9	45	43.9	
4						

3 Use the toolbar provided to amend the format of any chart element.

Chart object list · Format selected object · View datasheet · By column · Value axis (Y) gridlines · Chart type · Legend · Import file · By row · Category axis (X) gridlines · Display data table

`100%  Chart Area`

4 Click outside the chart to return to the main document.

Edit a chart

1 Double-click on chart to open it.
2 Amend/edit chart data or chart appearance as required.
3 Click outside the chart to return to the main document.

Insert an Excel chart

1 Open an Excel worksheet, and use Chart Wizard to create the chart.

2 Save the workbook.

3 Select and copy the chart.

4 Open the Word document.

5 Move the cursor to where you want the chart to appear.

6 Click 📋.

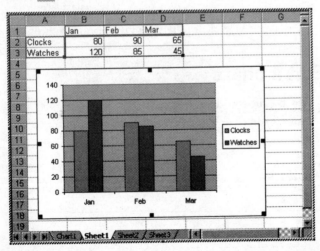

Edit an Excel chart

1 Double-click on the chart.
2 Use the Excel toolbar to edit the chart.
3 Click on the worksheet holding the data and edit it as required.
4 Click back to the Chart tab.
5 Click outside the chart to return to the main document.

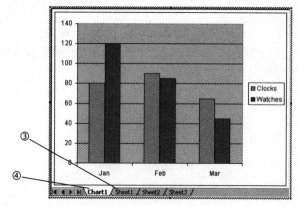

③
④

tip

To add a caption to a chart, see *Add a caption to a picture*, on page 160.

Insert a new Excel worksheet into a document

1 Move the cursor to the point in your document where you want to insert a worksheet.

2 Click 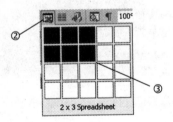.

3 Drag the mouse across the number of rows and columns to be included.

4 Click the mouse. The worksheet will be inserted.

5 Click outside the worksheet to close it and return to the main document.

2 x 3 Spreadsheet

Edit an Excel worksheet

1 Double-click on the worksheet to open it.
2 Amend/edit as required using the Excel tools on the toolbar.
3 Click outside the worksheet area to close it and return to main document.

Number formats

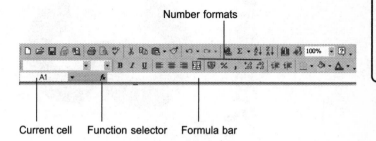

Current cell   Function selector   Formula bar

13

mail merges

Mail merges

If you want to send the same letter to a number of people, Word's mail merge facility allows you to automate many stages of the process.

You need two items to perform a mail merge:

- Main document (e.g. the letter that you want to send)
- Data source (e.g. the names and addresses of recipients)

In Word, you can either perform the whole mail merge operation in one go, using the Mail Merge Wizard. Or you can step through the process in stages using the buttons on the Mail Merge toolbar.

Create a mail merge letter and data source using the Mail Merge Wizard

1 Start a new document, and write the letter that you want to send. Do not type in any names or addresses at this stage.

2 In the **Tools** menu, point to **Letters and Mailings** and select **Mail Merge Wizard**.

3 Select **Letters**, and click **Next**.

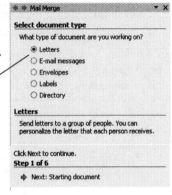

What type of document?

Which document to use?

4 Select **Use the current document** and click **Next**.

5 Choose an appropriate data source and click **Next**.

Who are the recipients?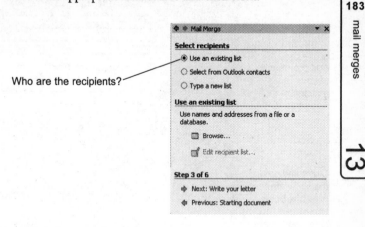

6 If you have selected to use an existing list, navigate to your data file, and click **Open**. Click **OK** when prompted.

7 If you have opted to **Type a new list**, click **Create**.

8 Enter the data (names and addresses) one at a time. Click **New Entry** to enter each new name and address.

9 Save the data list when prompted.

10 Click **OK**.

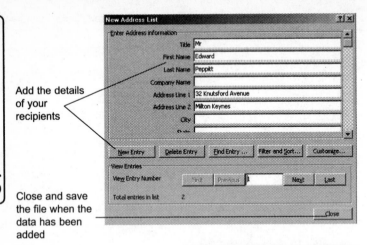

Add the details of your recipients

Close and save the file when the data has been added

11 Return to the letter, and use the tools supplied by the wizard to add the name and address data, as well as the way you plan to greet the contacts in your letter.

12 Click **Next** when you are finished.

Mail Merge

Write your letter

If you have not already done so, write your letter now.

To add recipient information to your letter, click a location in the document, and then click one of the items below.

  📋 Address block...

  📋 Greeting line...

  📮 Electronic postage...

  ▦ More items...

When you have finished writing your letter, click Next. Then you can preview and personalize each recipient's letter.

Step 4 of 6

  ➡ Next: Preview your letters

  ⬅ Previous: Select recipients

13 The Wizard will now preview your merged letters. If you are happy with the preview, click **Next**.

Preview at least a sample of the letters

The mailing list can be amended if need be

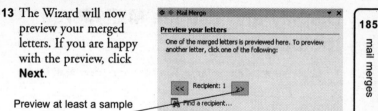

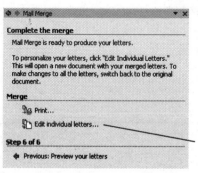

14 Complete the mail merge when ready.

Do any letters require special editing?

Display and use the Mail Merge toolbar

1 In the **View** menu, point to **Toolbars** and select **Mail Merge**.

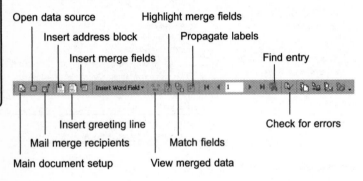

Open data source

Insert address block

Insert merge fields

Highlight merge fields

Propagate labels

Find entry

Check for errors

Insert greeting line

Mail merge recipients

Match fields

Main document setup

View merged data

Open a data source

Word can collect data for your mail merge from a table created in Word, an Excel spreadsheet or an Access database (as well as a number of other common file formats).

1   Open the letter or document that you want to merge.

2   In the **View** menu, point to **Toolbars** and select **Mail Merge**.

3   Click where indicated on the Mail Merge Toolbar.

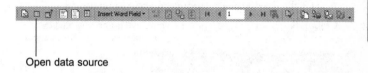

Open data source

4   Select from the **Files of type** drop-down menu.

5   Navigate to the file you wish to extract data from.

6   Click **OK**.

Edit a data source

You may want to add, remove, sort, edit or filter data in a data source before merging the data with your letter.

1 Click where indicated on the Mail Merge Toolbar.

Mail merge recipients

2 Amend the data source according to your requirements.

3 Click **OK**.

You can filter on any field by selecting the criteria for inclusion

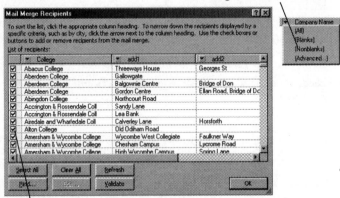

Clear the tick to remove from the mailing list

Specify where merged data will appear in a document

Ensure that the letter or document that you plan to merge is open and linked to the data source that you plan to use.

1 In the document, move the cursor to where you want to add the names, addresses or any other data.

Insert address block ———— Insert merge fields

Insert greeting line

2 Choose one of the three merge data icons.

3 Click **Insert Address Block** to add the address data to your document.

Set the address options

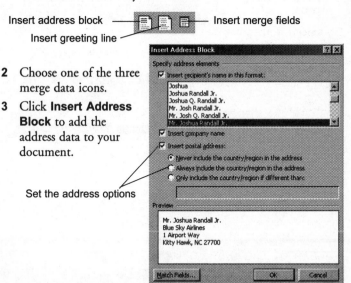

Insert Address Block

Specify address elements

☑ Insert recipient's name in this format:

Joshua
Joshua Randall Jr.
Joshua Q. Randall Jr.
Mr. Josh Randall Jr.
Mr. Josh Q. Randall Jr.
Mr. Joshua Randall Jr.

☑ Insert company name

☑ Insert postal address:

○ Never include the country/region in the address
○ Always include the country/region in the address
○ Only include the country/region if different than:

Preview

Mr. Joshua Randall Jr.
Blue Sky Airlines
1 Airport Way
Kitty Hawk, NC 27700

Match Fields...   Ok   Cancel

4 Click on **Insert Greeting Line** to select a greeting format.

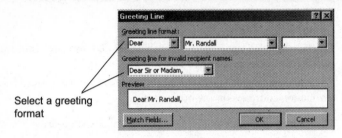

Select a greeting format

5 Click on **Insert Merge Field** to view and insert the complete list of available data fields.

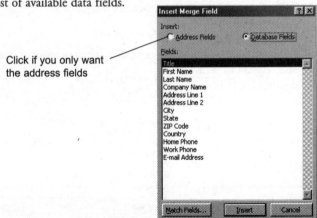

Click if you only want the address fields

Check for errors before merging

1 Open the letter that you wish to merge.
2 Make sure that the Mail Merge toolbar is displayed. In the **View** menu, point to **Toolbars** and select **Mail Merge**.
3 Click 🐧 on the Mail Merge toolbar.
4 Choose from the options presented, and click **OK**.

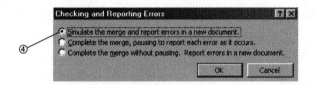

④

Checking and Reporting Errors   ? ✕

⦿ Simulate the merge and report errors in a new document.
○ Complete the merge, pausing to report each error as it occurs.
○ Complete the merge without pausing. Report errors in a new document.

OK   Cancel

5 Select an appropriate correction option for each error found.
6 Click **OK** when error check is completed.

Perform the mail merge

1 Click one of the merge icons on the Mail Merge toolbar.

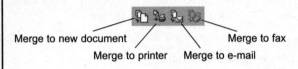

Merge to new document

Merge to fax

Merge to printer   Merge to e-mail

2 Specify which records to merge.

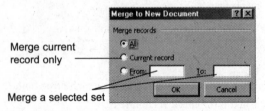

Merge current
record only

Merge a selected set

3 Specify what to do with blank records.
4 Click **Merge**.

View the mail merge before printing

Before you go ahead and print the merged document, you may wish to view how the letters look on the screen.

1 Click 🔳 on the Mail Merge toolbar.

2 Click ▶ to view each merged letter in turn.

3 If you spot any errors in the actual letter, correct them in the original document.

4 If you spot any errors in the names and addresses, correct them in the data source file.

5 When you are satisfied with how the letters look on the screen, perform the mail merge.

Merge address labels

You can use the Mail Merge Wizard to merge address labels using the same procedure as for a mail merged letter.

To perform the operation manually:

1 Open and save a new document.

2 Click 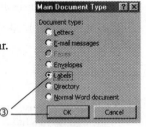 on the Mail Merge toolbar.

3 Select **Labels** and click **OK**.

4 Select mailing label type and printer information and click **OK**.

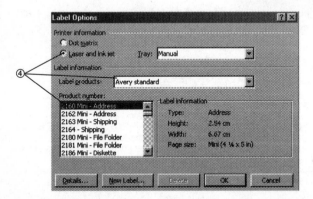

5   Click ▣ on the Mail Merge toolbar.

6   Navigate to the data file containing your names and addresses and click **Open**.

Now follow the instructions listed under **Specify where merged data will appear in a document** on page 189, and **Perform the mail merge** on page 192.

14

editing

Undo mistakes

1 Click  to undo the most recent action you have performed.

2 Keep clicking 🔄 to undo preceding actions one at a time.

3 Click the downward-pointing arrow to the right of 🔄 to view a complete list of actions that you can undo.

Restore an action you have undone

1 Click .

2 Keep clicking 🔁 to restore actions one at a time.

3 Click downward-pointing arrow to the right of 🔁 to view a complete list of actions that you can redo.

Find text within a document

In a large document, you can quickly lose a word, sentence or paragraph. The **Find** function will help you to locate it.

1 In the **Edit** menu, select **Find**.
2 Click on the **Find** tab.
3 Enter some/all of the text you are looking for.
4 Click **Find Next**.
5 Click **More** to broaden or narrow search criteria.

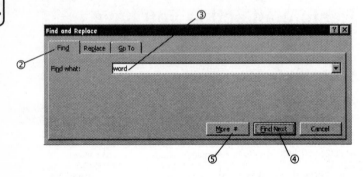

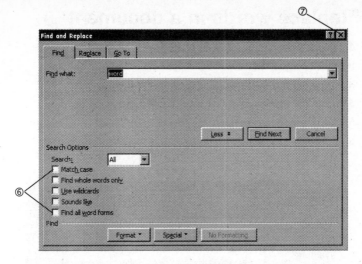

6 Set the options as required and search again.

7 Close the dialog box when you have finished.

tip

> You can search in part of a document only. Highlight the part
> of the text that you want to search in before starting the Find.

Replace words in a document

1 In the **Edit** menu, select **Replace**.
2 Click on the **Replace** tab.
3 Type the text to be replaced into the **Find what** field.
4 Type the replacement text into the **Replace with** field.
5 Click on one of the replace options.
6 Close the dialog box when the replacement is complete.

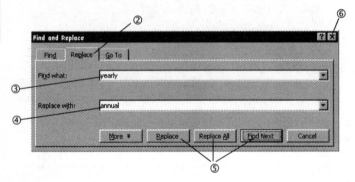

tip

Click ![undo icon] to undo the replacement quickly.

Go to a specific item

1 In the **Edit** menu, select **Go To**.

2 Select the type of object that you want to go to.

Either

3 Enter a page or other object number.

4 Click **Go To**.

Or

5 Leave the object number blank.

6 Click **Next** or **Previous**.

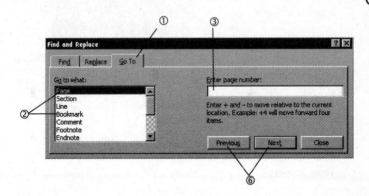

Add a page break

1 Move cursor to the point in the text where you want to insert a page break.

2 In the **Insert** menu, select **Break**.

3 Select **Page break**.

4 Click **OK**.

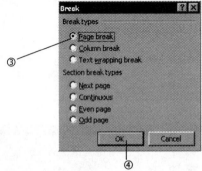

Remove a page break

1 Click ¶ to show paragraph marks.

2 Highlight the dotted page break line.

3 Press **[Delete]**.

Add a section break

1 Move cursor to where you want to insert a section break.

2 In the **Insert** menu, select **Break**.

3 Select the section break type.

4 Click **OK**.

Remove a section break

1 Click ¶ to show paragraph marks.

2 Highlight the dotted section break line.

3 Press **[Delete]**.

Change the type of section break

1 Click inside the section that you want to change.

2 In the **File** menu, select **Page Setup**.

3 Click on the **Layout** tab.

4 Select the desired **Section start** type and click **OK**.

Apply line numbering

1 In the **File** menu, select **Page Setup**.

2 Click on the **Layout** tab.

3 In the **Apply to** drop-down menu, select **Whole document**.

4 Click **Line Numbers**.

5 Tick **Add line numbering**.

6 Set the options.

7 Click **OK**.

8 Click **OK**.

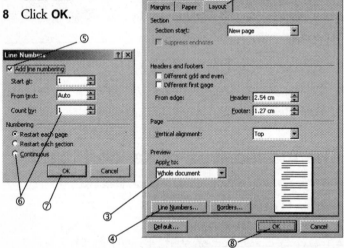

Create a table of contents

In order to create a table of contents automatically, it is essential
that you have used styles (e.g. Heading 1, Heading 2) within your
document. See page 75 if you require more information about
styles.

1 Move the cursor to the point in your document where you want
   your table of contents to appear.

2 In the **Insert** menu, point to **Reference** and select **Index and
   Tables**.

3 Click on the **Table of Contents** tab.

4 Choose a suitable format.

5 Click **Options…**

6 Select the styles to be included in the table of contents

7 Click **OK**.

8 Click **OK**.

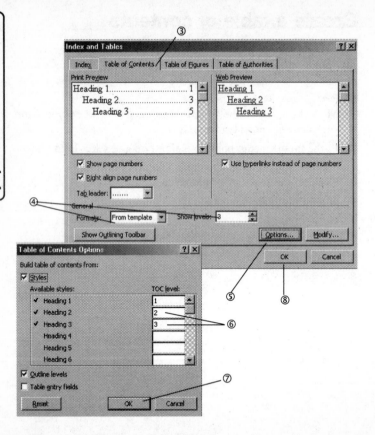

Update a table of contents

1 Edit the document that has a table of contents, and save the changes you have made.

2 Move the mouse pointer to the left of the first line of the table of contents.

3 Click to select the table of contents.

4 Right-click inside the table of contents, and select **Update Field**.

5 Make an appropriate selection where indicated.

6 Click **OK**.

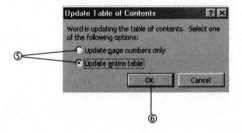

Create an index

First you must mark the entries for your index within your document.

1 In the **Insert** menu, point to **Reference** and select **Index and Tables**.

2 Click on the **Index** tab.

3 Click **Mark Entry**.

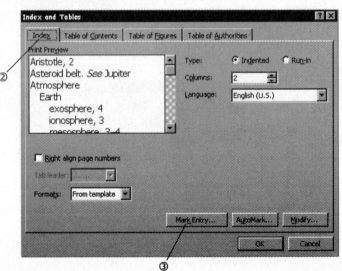

4 Highlight the first item you want to insert into the index.

5 Click in the **Main Entry** field to insert the highlighted word into the dialog box.

6 Select from one of the **Options**.

7 Click **Mark** (or **Mark All** if you want to insert all occurrences of this word/phrase in the index).

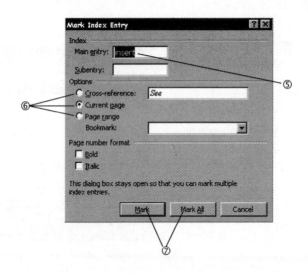

Add a page range to an index

1 Select the text within the page range to be included.
2 In the **Insert** menu, select **Bookmark**.
3 Enter a name for the bookmark, and click **Add**.
4 In the **Insert** menu, point to **Reference** and select **Index and Tables**.
5 Click on the **Index** tab.
6 Click **Mark Entry**.
7 In the **Mark Index Entry** dialog box, type in the **Main Entry**.
8 Select **Page Range**.
9 Select the bookmark name.
10 Click **Mark**.

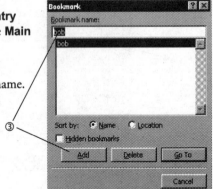

Compile the index

1 Click ⟳.

2 Close the **Mark Index Entry** dialog box (if it is open) and move the cursor to the end of the document.

3 In the **Insert** menu, point to **Reference** and select **Index and Tables**.

4 Click on the **Index** tab.

5 Select an index type and style.

6 Click **OK**.

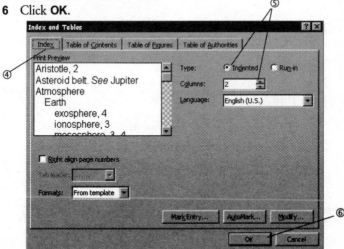

Track changes as you or your colleagues edit

You can track the changes that are made to a document.

1 Open the document that you want to track.

2 In the **Tools** menu, select **Track Changes**.

Word will track inserting, deleting or moving text or graphics. It will also track formatting changes.

Review changes and comments

1 In the **View** menu, select **Markup**. Changes will now be displayed for you to review.

This unit brings alive the amazing world of plants through time-lapse and high-magnification photography. Using the setting of the Botanical Gardens Birmingham Mr Rotivator provides children with an exciting view of plants as they grow, change, and reproduce.

> Deleted: From the humblest of urban weeds to the beauty of the British countryside
>
> Deleted: are given

2 Use the Reviewing toolbar to accept or reject changes, add comments, or choose which changes to display.

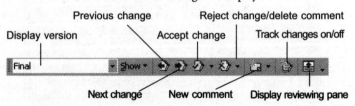

Display version   Previous change   Accept change   Reject change/delete comment   Track changes on/off

Final   Show ▾

Next change   New comment   Display reviewing pane

15

multiple documents

Open multiple documents

In Word, you can open and work on several documents at the same time.

With one or more documents already open:

1 In the **File** menu, select **Open**.

2 Navigate to the next document that you want to work on.

3 Click **Open**.

A new window appears containing this document.

You can also start a new document while continuing to work on another:

1 In the **File** menu, select **New**.

Or

• Click on

Switch between open documents

1 In the **Window** menu, select the document that you want to work on.

This document now becomes active. The other open documents are still available, but remain inactive until you select them in the method described above.

Cut/copy text between documents

In Word, you can cut, copy and paste between a number of open documents.

1 Open the document that you want to cut or copy text from.

2 Click or ▣ as required.

3 Open the document in which you want to paste the text.

4 Move the cursor to desired place in the document.

5 Click ▣.

tip

You can also switch between documents by clicking on one of the files listed on the taskbar at the bottom of the screen.

View several documents at once

In Word, you can view more than one document on your screen at the same time.

1 Open the documents that you would like to view together.

2 In the **Window** menu, select **Arrange All**.

Split the document window

You may wish to display two parts of the same document simultaneously.

1 In the **Window** menu, select **Split**.

2 Drag the shaded line into the desired position, and then click once to fix the line in position.

You can now scroll to different parts of the same document in each of the panes.

16

the web

Create a hyperlink to a web page

If you type a web address into a Word document, it will automatically convert it into a hyperlink.

You can also create a hyperlink manually, using the text of your choice to appear instead of the web address.

1 Move the cursor to where you want your hyperlink to appear.

2 Click on █ .

3 Type the text that will appear as the hyperlink.

4 You can add a screen tip (caption) if you wish.

5 Type in the web page address, or select it from the list of browsed pages.

6 Click **OK**.

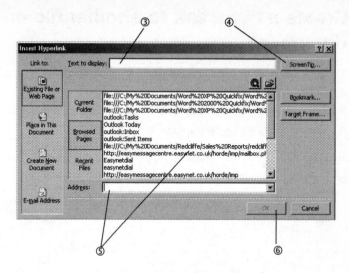

To go straight to my site, click here!

Hyperlinked text

Screen tip – appears
when the cursor is
over the hyperlink

Create a hyperlink to another file or document

1 Move cursor to where you want your hyperlink to appear.

2 Click on ![icon].

3 Type the text that will appear as the hyperlink.

4 You can add a screen tip (caption) if you wish.

5 Type in the file path for the document, or select it from the list of recent files.

6 Click **OK**

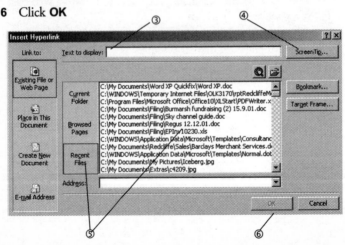

Save a document as a web page

Ensure that the document works satisfactorily as a web page by seeing what it looks like in Web layout view first. Click 🖪.

1 In the **File** menu, select **Save as Web Page**.

2 Navigate to a suitable directory and give your web page a name.

3 Click **Save**.

4 In the **File** menu, select **Web Page Preview** to view the document as a web page.

If Word warns you that converting your document into a web page will lose certain items, you can:

• Continue anyway and accept that the finished web page will not look exactly like the original Word document.

• Cancel the operation, return to Word, and modify the document before trying again.

Create a basic web page

Word comes pre-loaded with a number of web page templates, as well as a Wizard.

1 In the **File** menu, select **New**.

2 Select **General Templates** from the **Task Pane**.

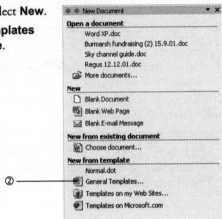

3 Click on the **Web Pages** tab.

4 Double-click on the web page template that you want to use.

5 Use the template as the basis for your web page.

6 Overwrite the existing copy with your own words.

7 Save your web page.

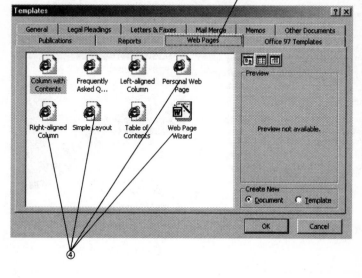

17

templates

Create a new template

1 In the **File** menu, select **New**.

2 Select **General Templates** from the **New Document** dialog box.

3 Click to select **Template**.

4 Click **OK**.

5 Enter text and features that will be common to all documents based on the new template, and format the text and layout as you want it to appear.

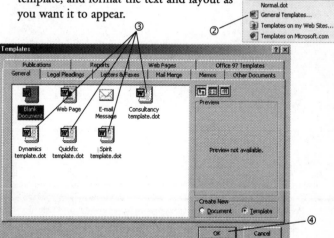

6 In the **File** menu, select **Save As**.

7 Choose a suitable name for your template.

8 Click **Save**.

Now you will be able to select this template whenever you select **New** in the **File** menu.

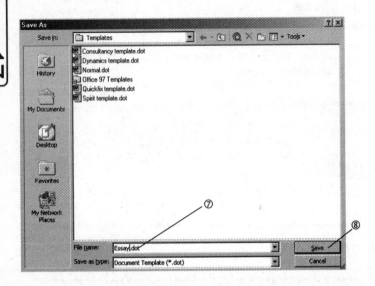

Modify an existing template

1 In the **File** menu, select **Open**.
2 In the drop-down menu, select **Document Templates**.
3 Navigate to template and select it.
4 Click **Open**.
5 Make any changes/modifications.
6 In the **File** menu, select **Save As** to save the modified template under a new name.

Or

In the **File** menu, select **Save** to save the modified template under its original name.

Usually templates are stored in the *Windows* folder, in a folder called *Application Data*.

Convert a document into a template

1 Open the document you want to use as a template.
2 In the **File** menu, select **Save As**.
3 In the **Save as type** drop-down menu, select **Document template**.
4 Name your new template.
5 Click **Save**.

Use a template

1 Click **Start**, and select **New Office Document**.
2 Navigate to the template that you want to use.
3 Click to select template.
4 Click **OK**.

18

text boxes

Create a text box

Text boxes use the same drawing canvas employed when you draw
pictures, lines or shapes (see pages 154–158). The drawing canvas
makes it easier to line up and place text boxes neatly.

1 In the **View** menu, point to **Toolbars** and select **Drawing**.

2 Click on 🖾.

3 Click and drag the mouse to draw text box.

4 The shape will be drawn inside a drawing canvas (see page 157).

5 Release the mouse button.

6 Click inside text box and start typing.

7 When you are happy with the text box, use the sizing handles
on the drawing canvas to shrink it so that it fits snugly around
the text box.

You can delete the drawing canvas altogether (see page 153).

Format a text box

1 Click on text box frame to select it.

2 Right-click and select **Format Text Box**.

3 You can format the size, colour and position of the text box.

4 Click **OK**.

You can align the text inside a text box. Click inside the text box and select one of the text alignment icons.

> The quick
> brown fox
> jumped
> over the
> big cow

Centre aligned

> The quick
> brown fox
> jumped
> over the
> big cow

Left aligned

You can also resize the text box. Click on the text box frame, and use the sizing handles that appear around the frame.

Create a text box link

You can flow text between two or more text boxes.

1 Click on the frame of the first text box.

2 Right-click and select **Create Text Box Link**.

Or

Click where indicated on the Text Box toolbar.

Our reason for writing this book is to share our experiences gained over many years of coaching people in a variety of companies. In this

Create text box link

3 Click on the second text box.

Our reason for writing this book is to share our experiences gained over many years of coaching people in a variety of

companies. In this book we present the structure that we use both in coaching our clients and as a basis for teaching coaching to managers and directors.

Previous text box   Next text box

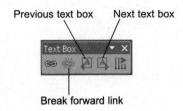

Break forward link

tip

To remove the link, right-click on the frame of the text box with the link and select **Break Forward Link**.

Make text flow sideways

1 Create a text box as described on page 230.
2 Enter the text and format the text box to your requirements.
3 Click where indicated on the Text Box toolbar.
4 Click outside the text box to deselect it.

Change text direction

19

help menu

Show the Office Assistant

The Office Assistant is an animated character that sits on your desktop. If the Office Assistant is running, help is available via the character's speech bubble. The Office Assistant will also offer tips and advice based on what you are doing in Word.

You can specify the way in which the Office Assistant provides help.

1 In the **Help** menu, select **Show the Office Assistant**.

2 Click on the **Office Assistant**.

3 Click **Options**.

4 Click on the **Options** tab.

5 Click to select the options you require.

6 Click **OK**.

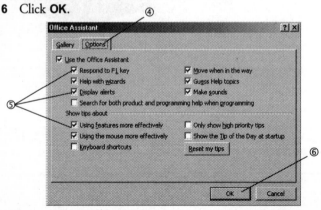

Use the Office Assistant

1 Click on the Office Assistant.

2 Type a question and click **Search**.

3 Select from the range of answers provided.

4 You will now be taken to more specific, detailed help.

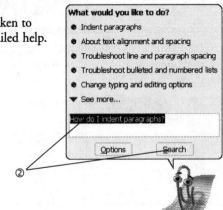

What would you like to do?
- Indent paragraphs
- About text alignment and spacing
- Troubleshoot line and paragraph spacing
- Troubleshoot bulleted and numbered lists
- Change typing and editing options
- ▼ See more...

How do I indent paragraphs?

Options   Search

②

tip

Try to make your question as precise as you can, otherwise you will not always find the answers you are looking for.

5 Keep drilling through progressively more detailed help until you find what you are looking for.

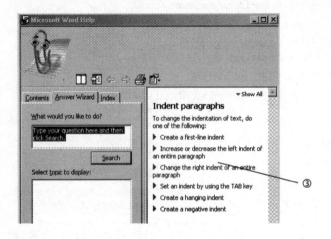

Turn off the Office Assistant

Many users find the Office Assistant irritating, and you may wish to turn this feature off.

1 Click on the Office Assistant.
2 Click **Options**.
3 Click on the **Options tab**.
4 Click once to remove the tick in **Use the Office Assistant**.
5 Click **OK**.

> You can also turn off the Office Assistant by right-clicking on the Office Assistant, and selecting **Hide**. But if you do this, the Office Assistant will return next time you open Word!

To switch ScreenTips on

1 In the **Tools** menu, select **Options**.
2 Click on the **View** tab.
3 Click to place a tick next to **Show ScreenTips**.
4 Click **OK**.

Use the What's This? command

1 In the **Help** menu, select **What's This?**

Or

   Hold down **[Shift]** and press
   [F1].

2 The mouse pointer will turn
   into a question mark.

3 Click on any feature within
   Word for a quick help sum-
   mary.

For example:

If you click on text, a panel
appears summarizing the font and
paragraph formatting.

If you click on a toolbar button, a
caption summarizes its function

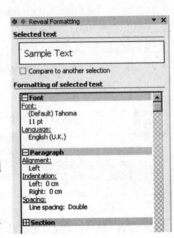

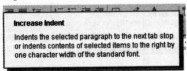

Use the Help command

The Help command is more useful if the Office Assistant is turned off (see page 239).

1 In the **Help** menu, select **Microsoft Word Help** or press **[F1]**.

2 Click on the **Contents** tab to see the range of help topics.

3 Double-click on a topic.

4 Select an individual query, and the help will appear in the preview screen on the right of the Help dialog box.

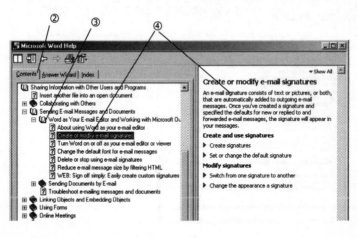

5 Click on the **Answer Wizard** tab if you have a specific question.

6 Type in the question and click **Search**.

7 Select a topic to display.

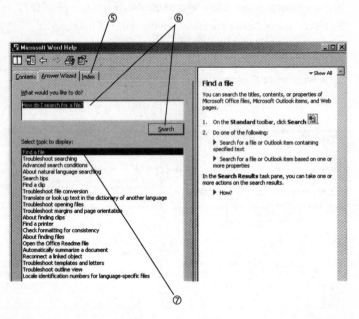